TENSIONS

H. A. Williams was born in 1919, and was educated at Cranleigh School and Trinity College, Cambridge. He trained for the priesthood at Cuddesdon College, Oxford, and was ordained in 1943. He held two curacies in London before becoming Chaplain and Tutor of Westcott House, Cambridge from 1948 to 1951. For eighteen years he was then a Fellow and Lecturer in Theology at Trinity College, Cambridge, being also Dean of Chapel for the last eleven of them.

He left Cambridge in 1969 to test his vocation with the Community of the Resurrection, Mirfield, Yorkshire, and was professed a member of the order in January 1972.

Harry Williams is the author of several books, including *Jesus and the Resurrection*, *God's Wisdom in Christ's Cross*, *The Four Last Things*, *Poverty, Chastity and Obedience*, *Some Day I'll Find You* (his autobiography), *True Resurrection* and *The True Wilderness* – the last three all available as Fount Paperbacks.

D0306394

£1.50

Books by the same author
available as Fount Paperbacks

Some Day I'll Find You
True Resurrection
True Wilderness

Available from other publishers

God's Wisdom in Christ's Cross
Jesus and the Resurrection
Poverty, Chastity and Obedience
The Four Last Things

Contributed to

Objections to Christian Belief
Soundings
The God I Want

TENSIONS

Necessary Conflicts in Life and Love

H. A. WILLIAMS

Collins
FOUNT PAPERBACKS

First published in Great Britain in 1976 by
Mitchell Beazley Publishers Limited
This edition first published in Great Britain by
Fount Paperbacks, London in 1989

Copyright © H. A. Williams 1976

Printed and bound in Great Britain by
William Collins Sons & Co. Ltd, Glasgow

CONDITIONS OF SALE

This book is sold subject to the condition
that it shall not, by way of trade or otherwise,
be lent, re-sold, hired out or otherwise circulated
without the publisher's prior consent in any form of
binding or cover other than that in which it is
published and without a similar condition
including this condition being imposed
on the subsequent purchaser

CONTENTS

'We can of course satisfy our logical needs by inventing mythic items or aspects which will each carry a distinct charge, but these correspond to nothing we can truly envisage. In this realm of exclusion and demarcation the religious spirit is plainly not at home: its deepest separations admit of the closest approximations, its remotest absences of the most intimate presence, its complete otherness of the deepest identification.'

J. N. FINDLAY, *Religious Studies*, June 1975

PREFACE

This book came to be written from the simple observation that everybody suffers from tensions of one sort or another, and that most people think that it shows something is wrong. The truth, I believe, is the exact opposite. There can, of course, be destructive tensions. But these are the exception. Most of the tensions we feel are a sign of health because they are a sign of growth. Such growing pains are not comfortable, but they are the price we have to pay in order to become more richly and satisfyingly our full selves.

I have tried to put this fact into the context of Christian living and belief. I did it first in a series of retreat addresses at Westcott House, Cambridge. These became the basis for *True Wilderness* a book published in 1976, and I am very grateful to Fount Paperbacks for issuing it.

The theme is, I believe, even more relevant today than it was twelve years ago. Corporate bodies no less than individuals suffer from tensions. Over the past decade the Church has become an obvious example. The existence of tensions in the belief and practice of the Church is often held up as showing a deep-seated malaise. It is in fact, I believe, a sign of the Church's vitality.

Far from indicating that the Church is on the road to becoming a spent force, such tensions show it to be very much alive and kicking. What we have to guard against is a kind of ecclesiastical hypochondria.

But this is not at all a churchy book. It is concerned with the personal experience of ordinary men and women which the Church, if true to itself, should reflect and embody.

When writing one can be aware of only the smallest fraction of what one owes to the ideas of others. But I am aware of being particularly indebted to the writings of W. H. Auden, Ian G. Barbour, G. Wilson Knight, Oscar Kollerström, and Rollo May.

I have recently come across a remark in a book by Father P. N. Waggett SSJE, published in 1905, which so well summarizes what I have to say that I will close this preface by quoting it: 'God is powerful on both sides of every pressure.'

H. A. WILLIAMS
House of the Resurrection,
Mirfield

March 1988

1

CONFLICT IS LIFE

In literature the hypochondriac has always been a figure of fun – Molière's *Malade Imaginaire*, for instance, or Mrs MacStinger in *Dombey and Son*, whose occasional spasms could be set right only by a large dose of Captain Cuttle's brandy. What the hypochondriac does is to mistake what is in fact the perfectly normal and healthy functioning of his body for something dangerously wrong. My heart beats fast because in the circumstances it needs to, but I imagine it is a symptom of heart disease. If, however, I am lucky enough to have a doctor who has the time and patience to explain to me how the human body works, then my heartbeats no longer disturb me. But that, of course, is not to deny that diseases do indeed exist and are widespread.

Now it is my belief that almost all of us suffer from a kind of psychical, spiritual, or perhaps we could say existential, hypochondria. We imagine something to have gone wrong when it is in fact inevitable and necessary. We mistake signs of health for symptoms of disease. One of the most widely disseminated forms of this kind of hypochondria centres round what we describe as tension.

People frequently talk about tension nowadays in the same manner in which piously helpful people once used to talk about sex. You will remember the sort of thing – the mastery of sex, living with sex, and so on, as if sex were a dangerous enemy which some brute or blackguard had inflicted upon the human race, instead of being one of the main sources of human vitality and joy. Tension is now given the same bad name as sex once was. It has to be endured, coped with, lived with, as if it were a misfortune. I am not denying that people can be – and sometimes are – torn apart by internal conflicts which are destructive. But I believe that, in general, people are caught up in destructive conflicts because they have failed to recognize those internal conflicts which are necessary, healthy and creative. Tension, in other words, is the price of life – a truth to which every new-born infant bears its unconscious but by no means silent witness. It is when we refuse to recognize and welcome tensions which are life-giving that we fall a prey to tensions which are death-dealing. That is why it is necessary for us to see through our hypochondria, and welcome what is healthy when we feel it.

Tension is coterminous with the universe itself. If I were a natural scientist I could describe to you the necessary tensions which manifest themselves in the realms of physics, chemistry and biology.

As it is, I have to accept it on trust that 'the smallest molecular particle gets its dynamic movement from the fact that it consists of a negative and positive charge, with tension – and therefore movement – between them'. The material world as we know it is the product of tension or conflict, and the material is here a pointer towards the personal, the human, and the spiritual.

The aim of this book is to describe some of the healthy, life-giving conflicts in which we are involved as moral and spiritual beings; or, in short, the conflicts in which we are involved in our relationship with God. If anybody made clear the necessity of such conflict, Jesus did. It was at the centre of his teaching, summed up in the warning 'I came not to send peace but a sword', or 'Whoever will save his life will lose it and whoever loses his life will save it'. In everything he said he made clear that there is no such thing as an easy, comfortable, placid relationship with God. If we think that there is and that we have attained to it, that merely shows that we are asleep or dead or, perhaps more accurately, simply as yet unborn. We haven't begun to be disciples of Jesus unless we know something, a very little, of the joy – with which he endured the cross.

Examples come easily to mind which will be gone into more fully later:

God is the ground of our being, the source from which we continually flow. Yet, while acknowledging our entire dependence upon God, there is a sense in which we have to fight for our independence over against Him in order that our individual personal identity may be established and confirmed. Therein lies the story of the creation and the fall, what the ancient liturgy of Holy Saturday describes as the 'necessary sin of Adam', and Adam of course is each one of us. We can grow in the knowledge of God and become full and effective people only if we are prepared to accept this conflict between dependence and autonomy.

Or again, there are generally not two but a hundred sides to every question. And this has very profound consequences in the realm of belief. If our beliefs are cut and dried, it means that we have anaesthetized ourselves against nine-tenths of reality. A faith which is life-giving and effective, a robust faith, has to be prepared to take doubt on board. It has to be prepared to accept the tension of competing truths so that we can say: 'Yes, that is the case. And yet *that* is also the case', and it isn't easy to see how the two things can be reconciled. What is nowadays called triumphalism is not the particular preserve of any church or sect. It is the cowardice which runs away from conflict under the disguise of a bogus assurance. Zeal, I believe, is generally the child of this bogus assurance. As Bertrand Russell said in 1949 about zealous communists: 'Zeal is a bad mark for a cause. Nobody has any zeal about arithmetic. It is not the vaccinationists but the anti-vaccinationists who generate zeal. People are zealous for a cause when they are not quite positive that it is true.'

Or, again, there is the ambivalence of love. The ability to love must involve the ability to hate. If I'm incapable of hatred I'm incapable of love. And because hatred is so unpleasant and disturbing an experience, people try to block off these vital areas of feeling in the name of commonsense or even of goodness, as though to be indifferent to somebody were a morally better state than hating them. I remember a character in one of Graham Greene's novels saying: 'I would rather have blood on my hands than water – like Pilate.' The fact is we can love God and our neighbour only at the expense of also being able to hate both of them. That is what Camus meant when he said that every blasphemy is a participation in holiness. Unless we are ready to entertain this conflict between love and hatred we shall never grow in the love of God or man. Drive the conflict underground and you deaden yourself, and your protest against your own deadness will manifest itself in neurosis, in one of those sterile destructive forms of tension from which we have to be healed and delivered.

Action, too, must bring its own conflicts. For to act means to choose to do one thing rather than another. It would be easy to act if by nature we were infallible or if we could fulfil every single possibility which presents itself to us. But neither of these conditions holds. We have always to act without fully knowing the consequences of what we do and without knowing what would have happened if we had done the other thing. Unless we are ready to receive this necessary conflict, we shall either be passive and do nothing (which is a bogus solution, since doing nothing is in itself a choice, choosing to do one thing – nothing – rather than another – something), or we shall be for ever blaming ourselves for having chosen to do what we *did* do (which is another destructive neurosis; from which, incidentally, we often hide by a false and therefore blatant self-confidence). Few people are sicker than the man of action who thinks he is certain he is right. His refusal of creative conflict makes him a prey to destructive forces.

There is also conflict in all knowledge, in all our acts of knowing. Kant pointed out beyond refutation that we can never by observation and thought know things as they are in themselves. For, in order to be able to observe it at all, we have to put what we observe in mental frames which belong to us and not to the object observed. Those frames are space and time. Without those frames our reason cannot function. And the frames do something to the things we observe, separate us from them, make them only partly themselves because they are also partly us – they are affected by the way we look at them. Thus the knowledge which unites us with our world at the same time also separates us from it. There is a fundamental split, an unbridgeable gulf, between the subject who knows and the object which is known. As intelligent beings we are therefore poised in the tension between union and separation. There are other tensions, too, in all knowing. The most obvious is that between the creative imagination on the one hand and the critical intellect on the other. The cold light of the discursive reason is in itself sterile and barren. The creative imagination is fecund and prolific, but it produces a great deal of nonsense as well as a great deal of sense. Like the lion and the unicorn, the imagination and the critical reason have to chase each other round the town.

Prayer, too, has its own tensions. I don't mean the struggle to be recollected, to quell what we describe as our wandering thoughts. That comes by our realizing that we are more than the thoughts which wander. I am referring to the conflict in our experience of prayer between personal encounter with God in a sort of I – Thou relationship, which is, so to speak, a private affair between myself and God, and the willingness to lose somehow one's own fixed personal identity in order to be made one with God's relationship to all creation. Intimately connected with this is the conflict between encounter and identification. What I mean is that in prayer we not only meet God. We also in some sense become God. We are swept into God's own reality as, to use the conventional words, the Holy Spirit prays within us. 'I live, yet no longer I.' In all prayer there is this tension between what could be described as the personal and the transpersonal. People's prayers go dead on them because of their failure to understand and accept the necessity of this conflict.

I have tried briefly to summarize some of the healthy life-giving tensions in which we are all inevitably involved. I have also hinted more than once that we fall a prey to neurotic destructive tensions because of our failure to recognize and accept those tensions that are healthy and creative.

God can remain for us no more than a breast to suck or a Big Brother who relieves us from the burden of being ourselves. Faith can be no more than a bigoted and blinkered adhesion to beliefs whose function is to keep us feeling cosy and safe. Love can be a disguised narcissism: we think it is God or our neighbour we see in the pool when all the time it is only ourselves. Action can be action for action's sake: the people or causes for whose sake we imagine ourselves active can be no more than ciphers whose real purpose is to give a boost to our own artificial self-image. Knowledge can be considered as a deceiver who never delivers the goods and leaves us in a state of complete scepticism and despair. Prayer can be either a sterile formality or a drug.

Life, however, is stronger than death. And if we refuse to let life in by the front door by accepting and welcoming those tensions which are necessary and healthy, life will sneak in by all sorts of back ways, establish itself in dark holes and corners, and bang about noisily and destructively within us. Because we have refused life with all the conflicts it inevitably involves, life will be against us instead of on our side. Or rather – and this is of cardinal importance – it will be against the perversions which masquerade as ourselves. That is a theme found frequently in the Old Testament: Yahweh will fight against His own people because they are not being authentically themselves – 'But they rebelled and vexed his holy Spirit; therefore he was turned to be their enemy and fought against them.' Just as physical pain is a warning that all is not well with us and something needs to be done, so neurosis is a similar warning. It is a call to repentance – not to repentance in its all too familiar garb of moralism and religiosity, but to real repentance: a fundamental change in our whole outlook and attitude, a radical reorientation of our lives, a new beginning which is like being born again.

In our hymns and prayers we are accustomed to pay homage to the life-giving cross, to the truth of losing our life to save it. Such sentiments can sometimes make us feel extremely pious – moved to the brink of tears as we sing 'When I survey the wondrous cross' and all that. The trouble is that we often fail to see what the cross tells us about life as a whole. In the New Testament the cross is more than once described as a conflict, as a creative conflict which leads to resurrection. The vocation of being human is a vocation to enter into that creative conflict and make it our own. It is true that to each individual person the call to conflict will come in a particular way. But behind that particular call is the general one to recognize and accept and welcome the life-giving cross in each and every department of our lives. Of that general human vocation I have tried to give a sketch by describing some of the conflicts by means of which alone we can become fully and rewardingly ourselves. And it is precisely by becoming fully ourselves that we can give glory to God so that He can look on everything which He has made and find it very good.

2

DEPENDENCE AND AUTONOMY

In Jewish rabbinic thought man was described as having a Good Inclination and an Evil Inclination. This looks as if it might have been no more than the trite observation that in man good and bad struggle for mastery. But in fact the rabbis were much more sensitive and subtle than that. I am not a Hebraist, but somebody who is has told me that in the Shema ('Thou shalt love the Lord thy God with all thy heart', etc.) the Hebrew word for heart occurs in the form spelt with two *beths*, and that many rabbis interpreted this as indicating that man is to love God both with the Good *and* with the Evil Inclination. This interesting hint is worth pursuing.

Clearly in rabbinic thought there is something extremely ambiguous about the Evil Inclination. First of all it is never doubted that God made it. Nor is it a matter simply of heredity; God implants the Evil Inclination directly in the soul of every individual at the moment of his conception or birth. Yet in his morning prayers the pious Jew asked – and still asks – God to guard him from the Evil Inclination: 'Lead us not into the power of sin, or of transgression or iniquity or of temptation: let not the Evil Inclination have sway over us.' The Law is often thought of as the antidote to the Evil Inclination: 'I created the Evil Inclination; I created for it the Law as a remedy. If ye are occupied with the Law, ye shall not be delivered into its hands.' One rabbi, in expounding the Genesis statement 'God looked on everything He had made and behold it was very good', says: 'Is the Evil Inclination then very good? Certainly, for without it man would not build a house, nor marry, nor engage in trade.' The question was sometimes raised whether the Evil Inclination was to be found in animals. One rabbi said that certainly it was, because animals bite and kick.

It looks as if what the rabbis called the Evil Inclination is something like what we call aggression, and they had too much insight and honesty to condemn it simply as evil. It was evil certainly from one point of view and one should pray to be delivered from it. But, on the other hand, it was created by God and was the source of man's own creative capacities. Without it man would not be man. And it was by means of his Evil Inclination, of his aggression, that man was to love the Lord his God.

Here we are approaching the first of those healthy life-giving conflicts summarized in the last chapter. We are entirely dependent upon God, yet at the same time there is a sense in which we must learn to be independent of Him. If we are to be truly alive, we must be ready in our relationship with God to accept the conflict between dependence and autonomy. Whatever Bonhoeffer intended, I think that it is in this sense that we must understand man's coming of age. It is not that in the twentieth century mankind has come of age in any evolutionary sense, but that it is God's will that a man should be fully himself; and that if a man is to be fully himself his relationship to God cannot find expression only or exclusively in terms of dependence. If I may once more borrow from the rabbis, they interpreted Jacob's wrestling with the angel at Peniel as his wrestling with God for a good covenant, for good terms. And because Jacob was not just passively dependent but took the appalling risk of wrestling with God for good terms, he got them. He was blessed 'for as a prince hast thou power with God and with man and hast prevailed'.

This insight was not unique to Jewish antiquity. You find it also in Greece. Much of Greek drama is concerned with that knife-edge between dependence on the powers that be and the necessity to assert one's own autonomy. Fall either side and you are destroyed. *Hubris* certainly is punished. But you can also fall a victim to mania.

In a nutshell the inner conflict we are concerned with is this: in order to be people and not ciphers we must needs fight that on which we rely.

What does this mean in practice?

Karl Barth once said very characteristically that

to call God 'Father' is not to speak of God anthropomorphically but to speak of man theomorphically. That is the sort of profound but crude statement allowed to prophets and poets, and Barth was both. The point is put, I think, far less strikingly but with greater finesse by means of the concept of analogy. In the relationship of human father and son there is something which reflects, points to, the relationship between God and man. We are used to the idea of analogy in the realm of thought. But we have emotions as well as intellects. We are beings who feel as well as think. And our feelings towards God are also a matter of analogy. That is to say, we do not feel God's impact upon us directly. We feel His impact upon us in terms of what we feel about human things. In the realm of feeling, God's impact upon us is a mediated impact. The sort of feelings evoked by parents, wives, friends, or whatever, are the necessary media or channels or vehicles of the feelings evoked by God. (And that, incidentally, is a very fruitful way in which we can consider the mystery of the Incarnation.)

What I have called the analogy of feeling can, for our purposes, be summarized thus: God impinges upon me in terms of the kind of feelings I have towards those human beings to whom I am closely connected. In the Bible people are described as the friends of God. In the Fourth Gospel Jesus calls the disciples his friends. And there is no need to remind you of the Old Testament picture of Israel as Yahweh's wife, or of St Paul's description of the Church as the Bride of Christ. But since God is the ground of our being, the fount from which we continually flow, since God is our origin, a great deal of our basic feelings towards Him will be channelled or conveyed to us by means of the kind of feelings which a son has for his earthly father. That is to say, the characteristic ambiguities, conflicts and crises which are part and parcel of a son's healthy and maturing relationship with his earthly father will inevitably find their counterpart in a man's relationship with God. As well as love and obedience, there will be resentment, rebellion and self-assertion – the bid, in short, for independence. Conflict of this kind is absolutely necessary if our relationship with God is to grow into maturity. And unless this absolute necessity is recognized, we shall misunderstand what is happening to us and be weighed down by an appalling load of guilt; or we shall repress the conflict so that it can find only a sneaking and perverted expression below the level of consciousness while we apparently remain God's good little boys, futile and ineffective half-people.

You may answer that I am speaking only of the temporary crisis of adolescence. But even on the human level I wonder how temporary the crisis in fact is? It is true that Dad probably soon ceases to be a threatening figure to be resisted, but the father-archetype is by no means confined to Dad.

Think of what some of you feel about the boss, or, if you are a clergyman, what you feel about bishops. Think of the pleasure with which, in democracies, the people vote against their rulers. Think of the anger generated by establishments of every kind. Even on the purely human level the crisis of adolescence seems to be active during most of our lives. On the deeper level, a man would have to be extremely conceited and blind to imagine he had outgrown his spiritual adolescence, that he was established enough as a person, that he was sure enough in his independence, completely to accept without conflict his entire dependence upon God. For that claim to be a full-grown man would be a claim to have reached the measure of the stature of the fullness of Christ, and to make such a claim would be in itself an indication of how bogus it is.

Our spiritual adolescence catches us up in a difficult contradiction. According to the laws of all growth, natural and spiritual, our deepest obedience to God our Heavenly Father will require of us the courage of disobedience. Our ultimate 'Yes' to God will require us to take the risk of saying 'No'. Our filial relationship with God, if it is to grow into a mature filial relationship, will confront us with the necessity of rebellion against Him. Hence the truth that it is the greatest sinners who make the greatest saints. And we have it stated in one of the most central expressions of Christian experience – the 'Felix Culpa' of Holy Saturday and the 'absolutely necessary sin of Adam'. If the doctrine of original sin is not a description of something which happened literally in the past, then what it does is to stress the inevitable tension in which we are all involved between an ultimate good and a temporary evil. Either we grow or we atrophy and die. If we are to grow, we must, like Jacob, fight that on which we rely. You can put this doctrinally as Tillich did by saying that the creation and the fall are synonymous.

You will see that I think the rabbis were on to something of fundamental importance when they said we have to love God not only with the Good Inclination but with the Evil Inclination as well. I am fully aware of the terrible risk this involves – ultimately the risk of losing one's life. But, if Jesus is right, you cannot save your life without being prepared to lose it. But the point I wish to stress is that willy-nilly, whether we like it or not, in our relationship with God we are bound to feel the contradictions and conflicts of our spiritual adolescence. In our own lives we are bound to feel the tension between the creation and the fall. Our obedience to God requires us to fight Him. And when we fail in that most radical and paradoxical kind of obedience people smell death in our churches and stay away.

This goes a long way to mitigate the apparent unfairness of human circumstances. One man has always been lucky, came from a good home, was educated wisely, was helped to fall on his feet and so on. Another man seemed never to have had a chance, he was bedevilled by misfortune from the start. But listen to these remarkable words of Martin Israel:

> Years can be spent in fighting against a multitude of misfortunes, and one's life can ultimately expire with a mumbled cursing against the whole cosmic process. Yet such a person may be nearer to the discovery of his own true being than one who is shielded against adversity by pleasant outer circumstances.

That is reminiscent of what I quoted from Camus in the last chapter – 'every blasphemy is a participation in holiness'. Respectability is not only a sociological phenomenon – suburban middle class and all that. Far more insidiously it is a spiritual phenomenon, a state of heart and soul. Whatever God wants in our relationship with Him it certainly isn't respectability. I imagine that the church in Laodicea treated God in the most respectable way. The divine reply to this treatment is invective worthy of youth at its most rebellious: 'I'll spit you out.'

I spoke of the risk we ran in loving God with the Evil Inclination. On the level of human relations sons do sometimes murder their fathers, while political leaders do sometimes get assassinated. But by and large the continuing conflict of adolescent rebellion only very seldom goes to those extreme lengths. In almost everybody the rebellion can be contained within manageable limits. The risk is there all right, and it is a real risk. But in general it is negotiated without much harm being done. And of course far greater harm follows from refusing to take the risk, for then you become a soured, ungiving, conventional and boring person – who else, in fact, but the Prodigal's elder brother?

The same patterns can be found on the level of our relationship with God. Some people show their rebellion against God by refusing to believe in Him. Determined atheists are invariably deeply religious people. Those who are atheists by purely and genuinely *intellectual* conviction are never determined atheists. As Cardinal Newman said: 'Those who are certain of a fact are indolent disputants.' The determined atheist, on the other hand, uses intellectual arguments as no more than a cover for his desire to kill God off, though he probably won't see through the trick he is playing upon himself. What I wonder is whether we can truly love God unless from time to time we disbelieve in His existence. I suspect that to love God with all our heart will sometimes, perhaps often, involve us in being atheists. We must not evade the conflict of our atheism. We must be ready to accept the tension of our discovery at certain times that we think the whole Christian bundle of tricks is a lot of bloody nonsense. The last thing God wants is 'yes-men', for a 'yes-man' is a far deeper denial of Him as creator than a man who can say 'No'. There are many interpretations of the words from the cross and I know my critical study of the gospels. But I would suggest that one possible line of interpretation is that it was precisely because Jesus had reached the point where he could say nothing else than 'My God, my God, why hast thou forsaken me?' that he was able afterwards to say '*Consummatum est*'. It was by his willingness at that point to become an atheist that he consummated his love for God.

Killing the father off, however, is only one form of the conflict. There is also sneering, ridicule, defiance, disobedience. Here our critical reason will seldom allow us to recognize what in fact we are doing. What I mean is that, granted our premises of belief, it is just absurd to sneer at God and ridicule Him. So instead we divert our anti-God feeling towards God-associated things: religious formularies and practices, pious people, our religious leaders, the Church, the Bible, and so on. Now please don't misunderstand me. All these God-associated things are relative, not absolute. And if they claim to be absolute they deserve to be told that they aren't. They are, all of them, ludicrously inadequate echoes of God, many of them downright caricatures. We may have to work for their restatement and reform. And meanwhile we can laugh merrily at the ludicrous contrast between God's reality and these attempted expositions of

Him. As Monica Furlong has said, in the last resort the only joke is the contrast between God and man. But laughter is not the same thing as ridicule. To be merry is not the same thing as to sneer. When we find ourselves sneering at God-associated things we may be pretty certain that the God-associated things are only a cover for God Himself. We often find that too shocking an admission to make to ourselves – are we sneering at Absolute Goodness? Or if not too shocking, then too absurd. We might as well sneer at the Alps. Yet in fact that is precisely what we are doing, not because we are doomed and damned and totally depraved, but because here on earth our sneering and ridicule is a necessary stage or element in our love for the Creator, who is leading us towards that independence of Him by means of which alone we can finally give ourselves totally to Him. The acceptance of our inevitable ambiguity towards God – with all the tensions, conflicts and guilt-feelings it involves – is part of that cross through which alone we can enter into fullness of life. What is really absurd and really blasphemous (since it defies the order of creation) is to imagine that we can love God without at times feeling highly aggressive towards Him. There is often more love in a 'Christ Almighty' than there is in a spiritually castrated 'Alleluia'.

Along with our aggressiveness towards God we have also to accept our aggressiveness towards our neighbour. It belongs to the nature God has given us to assert ourselves and to fight our neighbour. For only so can we begin to become our full selves and truly love our neighbour. Open honest selfishness generally does our neighbour far less harm than selfishness driven underground and appearing in disguise. It is more healthy to kick your neighbour for your own pleasure than for his own good. You will remember Bernard Shaw's injunction: 'Never beat a child except in anger.' There is a kind of integrity in open honest selfishness which is attractive because we are being given something genuine. In the moral and spiritual realm there is that which corresponds to social pretensions. I try to give myself and others the impression that I belong to the moral and spiritual upper classes when in fact I am very lower-middle-class, if that. We must always pray God to deliver us from spiritual snobbishness and its sanctified selfishness – our own or other people's. It was said of Randall Davidson that he was unscrupulous and power-hungry until he became Archbishop of Canterbury, when his moral and spiritual greatness came to the fore. Almost everybody needs to get somewhere, and to push himself to get there, for it is only after that successful self-assertion that he can begin to mature. Clerics are particularly susceptible to the hypocrisy of *Noli Episcopari*, because they refuse to recognize the inevitability of their continuing spiritual adolescence. Thus among us an amusing example of the first being last and the last first is the fact that when preferment is offered, mother upstairs packing is nearer to God than father in the chapel praying for guidance, because mother has accepted her need to love God with her Evil Inclination while father by his prayers is trying to disguise that need from himself.

I have given humdrum examples because we live in a humdrum world. But these sorts of occasion, which occur, if only in miniature, to all of us, are bound to activate at deep levels of our being the conflict of our fighting that on which we depend. Dependent for everything, for our very existence, upon utter self-giving love, we fight it by that self-assertion through which we must needs pass if ultimately we are to respond worthily to that love. And the stage of self-assertion is not in this life a temporary one. It remains as a permanent element of our selfhood. We do not pass through it gradually but steadily. Our maturity is a matter of fits and starts. At times we shall find that costly self-giving love is indeed a genuine expression of what we are. At other times we shall find the contrary. There is a wonderfully heart-warming letter which towards the end of her life the Spanish St Teresa wrote to a favourite friar. The friar had promised to go and see her but had been prevented by legitimate work. There is no holy resignation in St Teresa's reply to the friar's letter of apology. It is one long delightful and charmingly expressed grouse, such as might have been written by any woman of her education and literary talents. We love her for it and we love God, because she had the courage to be human.

But perhaps we shall not always be immersed in the humdrum. Perhaps either in ourselves, or in somebody we know, the inner conflict I've been describing will manifest itself to an epic degree. Those who have read Dostoevsky will know what I mean. For instance, it is the sensual profligate Dmitri Karamazov who in the end freely offers himself to suffer vicariously for the afflicted of mankind by going in exile to Siberia for a murder he did not commit. But this utterly self-giving heroism is possible only because he has first felt to the full the agonizing conflict between the compelling beauty of the spirit and the no less compelling beauty of the flesh. This is what he says (Sodom, incidentally, stands for profligacy in general):

Beauty! I can't endure the thought that a man of lofty mind and heart begins with the ideal of the Madonna and ends with the ideal of Sodom. What's still more awful is that a man with the ideal of Sodom in his soul does not renounce the ideal of the Madonna, and his heart may be on fire with the ideal, just as in his days of youth and innocence. Yes, man is broad, too broad, indeed. I'd have him narrower. The devil knows what to make of it. What to the mind is shameful is beauty and nothing else to the heart. Is there beauty in

Sodom? Believe me, for the immense mass of mankind beauty is found in Sodom. Did you know that secret? The awful thing is that beauty is mysterious as well as terrible.

What Dmitri here says of beauty is true also of evil. Evil is terrible but it is also mysterious. I'm not referring to the unsolved puzzle of how evil could have arisen in a world created by a good and omnipotent God, for on that topic Christians have written themselves out and have got no nearer a solution. I mean that evil by its nature is mysterious as well as terrible. Mysterious because, although evil is destructive and death-dealing, it must often provide the terrifying depths which men need to be creative. That is the agony, both as pain and the Greek *agon*, struggle, the crucifixion, which people of the deepest vision have to endure in order to find life and to give it. 'If my devils are to leave me, I am afraid my angels will take flight as well', as Rilke wrote to a friend in 1907. And most of us will know of William Blake's verdict that 'every poet is of the devil's party'. In the death-dealing quality of evil there is something without which, it seems, we cannot have an absolute fullness of life. It is the truth by which Milton betrayed himself in *Paradise Lost*, where, notoriously, Satan is the real hero.

Earlier in this chapter I used a psychological model, the relationship of a son to his human father. That model is here of no more use. In the mystery of evil we are up against one of those fundamental antinomies which we can only accept and can never explain. I mean that goodness can often in some sense require evil to give it wings, so that here we have a hint that the contrast between good and evil is not so absolute as we generally think. If we are to be really alive, I think we have to receive this ambiguity of good and evil. But we cannot receive it without stress of soul and severe inner conflict. I am not talking about the socially inevitable fact that we can seldom choose to do the ideal thing, our circumstances allowing us to choose only between two evils. That brings its own tensions, but they are more superficial. I am referring to the fundamental part which evil seems inescapably to play in the production of good – a terrifying fact from which much conventional Christian thinking hides by separating off redemption from creation as though the Redeemer were not Himself the Creator. That separation is a funk-hole which produces either deadness or that protest against deadness which is neurosis. Yet, as a matter of formal theology and inherited belief, we do admit that evil is the instrument by means of which goodness is supremely revealed and supremely effective. Judas Iscariot betrays Jesus, but the Son of Man goes thereby to his destiny as it is written of him. And for St John the judicial murder of Jesus is his exaltation. The men who crucify Jesus provide the context by means of which he accomplishes his work and is glorified. But familiarity with these ideas has bred in us, not indeed contempt, but a kind of reverential insensibility not unlike the sleepiness of the disciples in Gethsemane and on the Mount of Transfiguration.

It has been said that both good and evil are slain on the altar of beauty. And it is indeed the artist who gives us the most illuminating hint of how goodness and evil are ultimately one. Dante's *Inferno*, for instance, is not in fact the hell he purports to describe. As a work of art it is a masterpiece of majestic grandeur. Goya's *Witches' Sabbath* sets out to portray what has been fully accepted as hideous and repulsive, but it reveals some compelling treasure in that loathsome scene. Great works of art hint to us that Satan and Sanctus are one. But until we arrive at that vision in its fullness we shall remain in conflict upon our life-giving cross.

3

FAITH AND DOUBT

In this chapter I intend to talk about faith and the kind of inner conflicts it involves.

St Paul tells us that we walk by faith, not by sight. Sight stands for complete certainty, the absolute inability to doubt. People sometimes confuse faith with sight as though if faith were perfect it would be sight, as though perfect faith would consist of complete certainty, that absolute inability to doubt which belongs to sight alone. On this false assumption we may equate growth in faith with growth in certainty, and we may confuse growth in certainty with the anaesthetizing of our critical intelligence. If so, we haven't in fact grown more certain. We have only put to sleep the man within us who asks awkward questions. The result is either some form of disguised fundamentalism – what the Bible or the Church are supposed to say – or an irresponsible complacency which supposes that some clever thinker or scholar, unknown to us, has demonstrated that what we believe is true.

But the man within us who asks awkward questions is not so easily disposed of. We may have put him to sleep, but the sleeper can dream. In other words, we can drive the man within us who asks questions out of the living-room, but he won't leave the house. He will hide himself in the cellar of the unconscious. Our uncertainty will still be with us, not openly and honestly, but in the sneaking underhand form of a repression. And uncertainty or doubt repressed in the unconscious does the maximum of harm. One of the things it can do is to make us feel half-dead, so that all we ask of life is just the ability to keep going, to get through the routine as respectably as we can. Or repressed doubt can make us into yelling zealots, fascists of the spirit who think the noise they make is designed to persuade others while it is really designed to persuade themselves. Here the Middle Ages provide an obvious example. Conventionally they are described as the ages of faith. But in fact it was faith confused with sight, so that in the cause of certainty doubt was repressed. But it was not eliminated. It took the perverted form of torturing heretics and burning them at the stake, just as Hegel said of the Athenian people who killed Socrates: 'It was a force within themselves that they were punishing.' That is the secret of the *odium theologicum.* When controversy about the truth is loud-tongued, bitter and spiteful, there you have people desperately stifling their own doubts while they imagine themselves to be protecting the purity of their own faith. Nobody, I suspect, would get hot under the collar if some eccentric geographer began proclaiming that the world is flat, because in this matter science has given us authentic sight, not bogus faith.

Such then are the practical consequences of confusing faith with certainty so that doubt has to be repressed: lassitude, keeping going in a half-hearted and unrewarding way, or various shades and degrees of fanaticism. With luck the repressed conflict will lead to total breakdown whereby we somehow unconsciously *force* ourselves to face and receive what we have previously hidden away from, even at the cost of personal disintegration. And then we can start again from scratch because the old self *has* disintegrated. And that is genuine repentance which is always a dying to live, the homage of all we are to the life-giving cross.

But for most people the crisis is not dramatically concentrated in this way, just as for most people conversion is not a sudden catastrophic event. For most people dying to live is spread over the length and breadth of their lives, though generally in dozens of uneven heaps. In the realm of faith this means the acceptance of doubt as the healthy and inevitable concomitant of faith. 'No cross, no crown' means here 'No doubt, no faith.' A mature faith is always a battling faith in the sense that it is ready to accept and receive the discomfort or pain of conflict. And of course what we are here concerned with is not the correctness or incorrectness of theoretical beliefs, of theological ideas, but that on which we have staked everything, our life itself, our personal identity, everything we are, including our eternal future.

'Those who believe they believe in God,' wrote

the Basque Catholic writer Unamuno, 'but without passion in their heart, without anguish of mind, without uncertainty, without doubt and even at times without despair, believe only in the idea of God, not in God Himself.' A cardboard god, we might say, is much more comfortable than the real one. But then a cardboard god cannot give life, and the price of life is always conflict.

But we must not be misled by the word 'conflict' here. Doubt is not an enemy to be overcome. It is a friend with whom we need to live, a friend who gives to our faith the enrichment necessary for its growth, but who asserts his own rights in the house and can be a nuisance or even an agony. Perhaps we could find a parallel in the kind of stormy marriage where the couple are devoted to each other but express their affection by bickering. So must faith and doubt live together, providing a tension which is creative.

How, for instance, can you really believe in – and love – the God represented by and present in the Crucified, unless you have felt something of the intolerable mystery of evil? I spoke of evil in the last chapter and suggested that it might be seen, or fleetingly glimpsed, as providing the necessary context of good. But evil is not thus neatly and conveniently disposed of. It still remains as a gigantic negation of God, the denial at its acutest of goodness and love. Natural disasters like flood and earthquake destroy thousands, and leave thousands more to perish slowly in the worst possible misery. A child is born with the first embryonic stage of a mental disease which will slowly reduce him to a cabbage or ensure that his life becomes one long torture. You will remember the magnificent and desperate defiance of Ivan Karamazov:

> If the sufferings of children go to swell the sum of sufferings which was necessary to pay for the truth, then I protest that the truth is not worth such a price. I don't want harmony. For the love of humanity I don't want it. And so I hasten to give back my entrance ticket.

In a less passionate and more reflective mood, don't the biological and zoological sciences present us with the most terrible picture of the evolutionary process? I know that animals and insects do not have free-will and so are not capable of moral evil. But it is odd, to say the least, most uncomfortably odd, to find instinctual behaviour so ruthlessly concerned with its own survival whatever destruction must be wreaked on other species. One insect paralyses but keeps alive other insects in order to provide fresh food for its young. And it isn't always a question of survival. It is for fun that the cat plays with the mouse. I know that the cat can't sin and that it is doubtless anthropomorphic to describe the cat's fun as sadistic. But if the universe has been created by a good God and is supposed to reveal His glory, if, in St Paul's words, God has shown His invisible nature to be clearly perceived in the things which have been made, isn't it frighteningly strange that the created order should so often completely contradict everything we believe God to be? What of God's glory is revealed to us by cat and mouse? A favourite verse of mine from the psalms is, 'The lions roaring after their prey do seek their meat from God', but I wonder what appeal it would have for me if I myself or somebody I dearly loved were the meat.

In short, the created order doubtless reveals to us something of the God and Father of our Lord Jesus Christ. But it also denies Him. When the mighty fact of evil is not ignored or evaded it is bound to lace with doubt whatever religious convictions we imagine ourselves to entertain. And the initial questions – how can nature be red in tooth and claw and so totally indifferent to human suffering? – is the first step to that ultimate question: 'My God, my God, why hast thou forsaken me?' Upon the cross there was no sophisticated rationalization about the foolishness of God, but the simple and suffering acceptance of plain destructive contradiction. Yet – here is the Christian paradox – it was precisely through and by means of the simple and suffering acceptance of destructive contradiction that there was achieved that fullness of knowledge where knowledge and life are one and the same. As man, it was through the grave and gate of *doubt* that Jesus passed to his risen and indestructible knowledge of God. And that is the pattern for us too, as for all men. As George MacDonald wrote:

> The man that feareth, Lord, to doubt,
> In that fear doubteth thee.

In practical terms this means that we must be loyal to the totality of our experience and accept the fact that it certainly won't fit together in any satisfying scheme of logical coherence. Of course we must always try to fit together as much of our experience as we can, try to make sense of as much as we can, always striving for some sort of coherence, but at the same time we must be ready for our experience to confront with irreconcilable contradictions, so that often in the same breath we shall have to say of the same thing, 'Yes, it is true' and 'No, it isn't true'. When, for instance, we are told that there is a special providence in the fall of a sparrow, part of my experience tells me it is true and part of my experience tells me it isn't. That is the cross of faith. And at this point we are all apt, like the first disciples, to forsake Jesus and flee by evading or smothering that part of our experience which tells us it isn't true. But real faith, as Jesus showed us on Calvary, consists in accepting the 'No, it isn't true', thus recognizing doubt as itself an essential and important element of faith. And I mean real doubt, existential doubt about our own nature and destiny, doubt about where and what we are and where we are going. When we say of ourselves 'Yes, we are' and 'No, we aren't' it is often impossible for us to tell which of the two statements is the truer.

Failure to understand that cross of faith has led in Christian history to a great deal of barren wrangling, of which the most notorious example is the controversy about predestination and free will. It has now been transferred from theology to psychology. Are we the victims of our hidden compulsions or are we free agents? I believe we are both at the same time, and my experience has given me little confidence in the many attempts to divide the areas of compulsion from those of freedom. Were the people who crucified Jesus without sin because they knew not what they did?

If doubt is part of faith, it follows that agnosticism, not knowing, is also part of faith. Those who admit that they don't know are often stigmatized, especially by the church press, as wishy-washy and ineffective. Perhaps in the short run they are ineffective if being a Christian means being a recruiting sergeant or getting people to vote for your particular religious party. But in the long run those prepared to admit that there is far more they don't know than they do can be much more effective than others. In an autobiographical passage Albert Schweitzer wrote of his experience of preparing young people for confirmation when he was a Lutheran pastor in Germany. Most of his colleagues gave to their young people the impression that Christianity explained a great deal about this world and the next. Schweitzer emphasized that Christianity explained very little indeed, that most was unknown. Then came the First World War. On the whole, Schweitzer says, the young men who had been told that Christianity gave most of the answers returned from the trenches having given up religion altogether, while those who had been warned that Christianity explained very little returned as still practising Christians. It was the pastor who not only admitted but did nothing to disguise his own cross of faith who in the long run was the most effective. If people are truly to share our faith, we must allow them also to share our doubt and the agnosticism which is its inevitable corollary. We must be ready to admit freely that there are important areas of Christian experience which contradict other important areas. We have already noticed predestination and free will. As another example we could cite the Christian evaluation of history. We are often told that Christianity takes history seriously. We hear a lot about God acting through His mighty works in history, and so on. But the fulfilment of all things is not, so Christians believe, within history at all. It is beyond history in the new heaven and new earth of the Apocalypse. If God works in history we might reasonably expect the historical order to become better and better. But that is not the pattern. The pattern is death and resurrection. The world has not noticeably changed for the better since what is called the Incarnation. Hence A. E. Housman's taunt about 'the hate you died to quench but could but fan'. Christian experience thus both affirms the historical order and denies it. Failure to understand that particular cross of faith leads to fruitless controversies between those who champion secular Christianity, holy worldliness and so forth, and those who champion other-worldliness. When Charles Gore was once staying with the old Lord Halifax, the Viceroy's father, Gore and the other guests spent a long time discussing the rights and wrongs of a contemporary dock strike. Halifax was silent. But the time came when he could bear it no longer. 'What are you making the fuss about?' he asked. 'Isn't it all going to be burnt up in the end?' That scene dramatically illustrates a real tension of faith.

There are other kinds of tension as well, not perhaps quite so basic as having to say Yes and No at the same time, but none the less important and costly.

There is, for instance, the tension between commitment and enquiry. We have to scrutinize, criticize, sometimes even attack, what we love and value most in the world. That was the cross which Victorian Christians had to endure with regard to the Bible. In the middle of the nineteenth century the authors of *Essays and Reviews* – a book largely of critical essays about the Bible – were described as the 'Seven against Christ'. Later in the century Charles Gore's essay in *Lux Mundi* broke Liddon's heart. There were two sets of people who refused the cross of faith. One set consisted of those who gave up Christianity altogether. The other set consisted of those who blocked their ears to everything contemporary science and scholarship had to tell them about the Bible. The one set abandoned commitment. The other refused enquiry. Christians today owe everything to those who accepted both commitment and enquiry and were courageous enough to bear the cross which that double acceptance involved. That particular battle has now long been over. But there are contemporary ones. I suggest that one of the double acceptances required of us today is beginning to centre round the figure of Jesus of Nazareth. I hear, among the self-styled orthodox, the same kind of noises being made about scholars such as Professors Maurice Wiles and John Hick as were made in the past about the magnificent seven dubbed the Seven against Christ. Some will abandon commitment to Jesus. Others will refuse enquiry, taking the view that Nicaea and Chalcedon have said the last word. But the living Christian future will belong to those ready to accept both commitment and enquiry in spite of the very great discomfort brought by the tension between the two.

Parallel to commitment and enquiry, though different, is the tension between traditional values and prophetic insight. I don't think we can shut either of them out of our house, however much they scrap. For each of them the prevailing temptation is self-righteousness. Those who are exclusively concerned to defend traditional values and those who are exclusively concerned with throwing them to the winds in the name of prophetic insight have at least this in common: the moral indignation with which they receive criticism is matched only by the moral recklessness with which they inflict it. That is a sign that each party, the traditionals and the prophetics, are repressing within themselves forces which are advocating the other side. The traditionals are repressing the strong appeal of new vision, while the prophetics are repressing the guilt they feel in throwing overboard what is hallowed by age. That of course is a phenomenon by no means confined to religion and theology. It is equally true, for instance, in the arts (and among academic economists), where a new idiom in painting, sculpture or music has invariably at its first appearance been condemned by the aesthetic establishment as a blasphemous heresy (and academic economists have little to learn about heresy-hunts). By temperament, some of us are traditionals and some prophetics. There is no reason why either temperament should despise the other, but each must fully accept the cross of faith and be ready to be pulled in two ways at once. The traditionals must fully accept what for them is the secret and dangerous fascination of new prophetic insight. And the prophetics must be prepared fully to acknowledge to themselves, if not to others, how much they owe to the tradition. In each case there will be a load of irrational guilt-feelings which must be manfully borne and not evaded or driven underground. The traditionals will feel guilty for being fascinated by the dangerously new ('it was a force within themselves that they were punishing'). The prophetics will feel guilty (as we have seen) for criticizing and discarding the old and accepted. Only when each is ready to bear his particular cross will the tension between the two be creative. In our own age one of the great signs of God's presence with His people is the way in which, since Vatican 2, the Roman Church has recognized and accepted this aspect of the cross of faith. And the process was initiated by a pope who by temperament was one of the most traditional of men. For was not Pope John reprimanded by the *Church Times* itself because as a personal preparation for the opening of the council he went on pilgrimage to the Holy House at Loreto? I hope that one day the angels will repay us for all the fun we must give them.

You must be prepared for what began as prophetic insight to become part of the hallowed tradition. T. H. Huxley said that new truths begin as heresies and end as superstitions. That happens in our own lifetime. What I mean is that the new prophetic truth you champion when young will be slowly incorporated into the traditional values. And you will one day wake up to find yourself considered terribly old-hat by younger people who have seen aspects of the truth to which you were – and are – blind. This discovery by a poacher that he has become a gamekeeper has its amusing side

– perhaps we could call it the lighter side of the cross of faith. If we are unprepared for it, it means that we haven't understood that truth is dynamic, that it will never sit still and stay where it is, but is always on the move, *not* getting ever fuller and more comprehensive so that our knowledge of the Eternal is more accurate, deeper and more complete than that of our forefathers, but dancing about, shedding light first in this place, then in that, then in the other. Truth for us is like a spotlight, not a floodlight.

The tension of faith is one of the most exciting and stimulating things life has to offer. Once again let us recall the joy set before him with which, the New Testament tells us, Jesus endured the cross. As we have seen all along, faith has its very grim side 'for the Word of God is living and active, sharper than any two-edged sword, piercing to the division of soul and spirit, of joints and marrow, and discovering the thoughts and intentions of the heart'. But, for all that, faith is also fun. 'Shall I, a gnat which dances in Thy ray, *dare* to be reverent?'

4

KNOWING AND
NOT KNOWING

In the last chapter we considered the inner conflicts which are part and parcel of all genuine faith. This chapter will be concerned with the act of knowing, how we know, and the inevitable tensions which belong to our ways of knowing.

Whatever it is we seek to know, our way of knowing it involves contradiction. For in order to know anything we have to put it into the mental frames of space and time, so that the object known is only partly itself because it is also partly the way we look at it. What we know, therefore, is not the thing in itself but the thing as it appears to us, so that our knowledge of a thing not only unites us to it but also separates us from it. Our knowledge is in part veridical and in part imaginary. It consists, as Wordsworth put it, of what we half create and half perceive.

If that is true with regard to earthly things, how much greater is the degree of contradiction, the swing between unity and separation, which is involved when we are concerned with heavenly things. Like all other intellectual disciplines, theology must try as best it can to describe what is in fact the case. It must be concerned with what is there, with Reality. But in its attempts to describe

Reality, theology is up against a fundamental difficulty. The Reality theology attempts to describe passes infinitely beyond the range of earthly things. But it is only in terms of earthly things that we can speak or think, so that when we set out to speak or think of heavenly things we have to do so in terms which are earthly. The result is that our descriptions, to ourselves in our own mind or spoken to others, both inform and misinform at the same time. That is the cross of our theological understanding, and it has been recognized by Christian thinkers almost from the start. But what was clearly perceived by a Clement of Alexandria, a Cappadocian Father, a Maximus the Confessor, a St Thomas Aquinas, and so on, is easily forgotten in the rough and tumble of the Church's life. And the consequent demand is made that established Christian doctrines be treated as if they were photographs of Reality, and theological thinking be tested and judged by the degree of accuracy with which it reproduces the photographs. Englargements of some particular detail of a photograph are allowed, and indeed encouraged, but the enlargement must faithfully reproduce what is portrayed, albeit minutely, in the original. And when it is objected that an established Christian doctrine is not a photograph of Reality at all, but of necessity no more than a collection of hints about Reality which both inform and misinform at the same time, the cry generally goes up that Christian thinkers are losing their nerve in the face of contemporary scepticism, that they are guilty of the *trahison des clercs*, and so forth, as if Clement of Alexandria and the rest had never lived at all. Such accusations are particularly ironical when they centre round the death and resurrection of Jesus, since those here accused of denials and scepticism are often precisely those who in the confidence of resurrection are accepting the cross in their theological thinking, while their accusers are in their thinking only watching the cross from afar in an uninvolved security. But the security is bogus. For in the realm of knowledge, as everywhere else, to be invulnerable is not to be immortal. It is only to be dead.

There is a dead deadness and a living deadness. Dead deadness makes Christianity irrelevant, as though it had nothing of significance to say about anything. Living deadness plays upon people's sickness. By those whose neurotic compulsions force them to close themselves up against nine-tenths of life, living dead Christianity is clutched at with frantic eagerness because it provides them with a still bigger and better neurosis, not only leaving them safe with their obsessions, but conferring on their obsessional maladjustments a halo of apparent sanctity. It is as though Jesus had never been concerned to heal the sick, but only to get them to accept an ideology whereby their sickness could be safely maintained by being projected upon the heavens. Success, in the sense of attracting crowds, is no guarantee of validity and truth.

Hitler attracted crowds, while, as far as Jesus was concerned, the gospels seem to indicate that the crowds fell away and deserted him, finding the truth he proclaimed too difficult to take.

I have laboured this point because here and there I occasionally see signs that some Christians are passing from dead deadness to living deadness and imagining it is resurrection. We shall avoid that mistake if we are willing to receive the cross in our thinking, feeling the discomfort or pain of inner conflict in our theological knowledge and recognizing it as the kind of tension which brings life.

Our doctrines are not photographs of Reality. They are the attempted description of heavenly things by means of the hints and guesses which earthly things provide.

In the Christian past this fact was put out in three main forms. There was the way of negation, what the Eastern Orthodox describe as the apophatic method: roughly, you say in the same breath that something both is and isn't. There was the way of analogy which the schoolmen endeavoured to refine into what they believed to be almost a precision instrument: God could not be described directly. But in earthly things and earthly relations there was that which in some way or other corresponded to the Divine and its relation to the world. The crux here was the 'some way or other' of the correspondence, so that the argument turned upon the question: In what way? And there was the way of paradox, favoured by the Reformed tradition. The

Divine could be described only in terms which were apparently contradictory because our thought is earthbound. God's wrath, for instance, is paradoxically the same thing as His love. It is only the limitation of our human vision which makes them seem opposites.

These three traditional ways of theological thinking can doubtless still be used with great fruitfulness. Eastern Orthodox thought rings bells for many people, and so do the neo-Thomists and the Barthians. There is an important place for schools of this kind. Our theological thinking would be immeasurably poorer without them. But in the last resort theology cannot be the special preserve of an in-group. It must be able to convey its truth to all with open hearts and open minds. And the ability to communicate with others, if you like with outsiders, is not only – or chiefly – for their benefit. For we ourselves can evade or falsify the fullness of Christian experience by reducing it, or encapsulating it, within the thought-patterns of our favourite school. The task of communicating Christian experience to outsiders forces us to enlarge our perspective and think things out again. In order that others may understand, we ourselves have to understand better. What Cecil Day Lewis wrote about poets is true of theologians:

> We write in order to understand, not in order to be understood; though, the more successfully a poem has interpreted to its writer the

meaning of his own experience, the more widely will it be understood in the long run.

That means that we must interpret Christian experience for ourselves as belonging to our own age and generation. Procedures belonging to the past are informative and stimulating, but we must make them our own. And because we belong not to the past but to the present, the procedures of the past will have to be reorganized and reinterpreted and restated.

So for us today the cross in our theological thinking cannot be simply a matter of negation, or analogy, or paradox. For while this world lasts the cross is always contemporary. To treat the cross as no more than a past event, or the resuscitation of a past event, is to evade it.

What, then, today is the cross of theological understanding? If doctrines are not photographs of Reality, how today can they be considered?

We have first to take into account what the sociologists have shown us. The fact that some sociology is superficial and glib, and its conclusions no more than the refracted image of its own procedures, should not blind us to its well-authenticated discoveries. These have been particularly illuminating in the sphere of knowledge. With a wealth of substantiating evidence the sociologists have shown us that our knowledge is not a matter of seeing with clear, innocent and unconditioned eyes. Our whole collective history, our whole culture, our whole style and manner of life, impose spectacles upon our eyes, and it is through those spectacles that we look at things and assess them. Those spectacles are the medium of our knowledge. Thought does not move autonomously in a social vacuum. It is always in large part the product of the social context in which it thrives. To some extent, of course, that is not news to Christian thinkers. Most of us have always understood, to take a random example, that Anselm's doctrine of the atonement was conditioned by the feudal society in which he lived. But, on the whole, we have restricted the application of this sociological insight to matters like the atonement, where a great deal of liberty of interpretation has always been allowed. I believe we have now to apply it to areas where interpretation has been more fixed. To ask a question: 'How meaningful is it still for us to think of God or Christ in terms of a sovereign Lord and Master?' To see how meaningful that concept once was you have only to read the preface to the Authorized Version and notice the way in which King James the First is addressed, 'most dread sovereign' and so on. And I suspect that up to the Second World War the organization of society was still at least felt to be hierarchical, so that the sovereign at the top of the pyramid was still as good a picture as any of Almighty God. Has the situation now changed? Are people any longer emotionally committed (by way of acceptance or reaction) to the idea of hierarchy? If not, how long will it still be meaningful, if indeed it still is, to think and talk of God as Lord and King? Could it be that the reaction of the learned to John Robinson's *Honest to God* was naïve in the extreme? Of course the book was a ragbag of second-hand theology and philosophy (an infinitely better ragbag, incidentally, than the present book). But was the fact that it sold in millions attributable to the hope it offered that belief in the Divine was not chained for ever to pictures whose sociological significance was outworn and which were therefore lifeless?

Whether or not that was so, the sociology of knowledge shows us an important part of the contemporary cross of Christian understanding. We can think and speak of God, who by definition is absolute, eternal and unchanging, only in terms which are relative and ephemeral and highly conditioned by the society and culture in which we live. What, therefore, looks (and to many feels) like treachery and disloyalty to Christian truth may in fact be the highest form of loyalty to it, enabling it to have life and to prevail by restating it in terms which are sociologically contemporary – that is, in terms of the mental and emotional air in which we live and move and have our being.

In this connection Dennis Nineham has made a most interesting suggestion.

Let us for a moment imagine, [he says] that immediately after its completion, the sole text of the Bible was lost until its discovery in a cave near the Dead Sea some few years ago. In that case, however deeply impressed modern readers might have been by the newly discovered text and however much they may have pondered over it, they would never have constructed on the basis of it anything like those essentially late-Hellenistic constructions, the doctrines of the Trinity and the Incarnation.

We can answer what Nineham would certainly allow: that in fact we cannot step out of history and escape being products of the historical process, the Christian past having things to teach us of vital importance. But what he has underlined is that doctrinal formulations, even the most prestigious and hallowed, are relative, not absolute. And if they are to say to people today what they said to people in the past, they may have to be changed fairly radically. To express the unchanging in terms which themselves change is the inner conflict, the cross of Christian knowledge. And it will present itself not merely as a change in decoration or frills, but as a change in substance. In the rhythm of cross and resurrection it is the change in substance which gives life to our apprehension of the abiding Reality. The alternative is death – dead death or living death.

Abandoning the photographic view of Christian knowledge will today lead us to the consideration of models. For we live in a scientific age, and natural science has taught us to think in terms of models. I am not a scientist, as I belong to the one-culture age. But I understand that in science theoretical models are not taken literally. They are not literal pictures of reality (photographs), but neither are they useful fictions by which we pretend for convenience's sake that such-and-such is the case. In science, theoretical models are partial and provisional ways of imagining what cannot be observed or otherwise reached. So, for instance, I am told that gases are understood according to the model of their being composed of tiny elastic spheres, though it is admitted that the model bears only a partial resemblance to what it attempts to describe and thus remains hypothetical. But being as good a description as has been so far possible, scientists consider it worthy of at least a tentative commitment.

Christian doctrines are like the theoretical models of science. They are neither literal pictures nor useful fictions. Christian doctrines are not a game of 'Let's pretend that so-and-so is the case in order that we may lead better and more loving lives'. They are an attempt to describe what is really there by the best models available at any time. But the models can provide only partial and inadequate descriptions, and they may speak meaningfully to one age and not to another. And because they are models of this kind Christian doctrines are by nature only hypothetical, and the commitment we can give them is thus only tentative. Doctrines cannot escape reformulation as society changes, just as scientific models cannot escape reformulation as scientific attitudes change. In their form, therefore, creeds are as tentative as scientific hypotheses. The Reality to which they point and attempt to describe does not, of course, change. The difficulty is to distinguish between the unchanging Reality and the changing formulation, to recognize that the Reality does not depend upon the attempted formulation of it. Facing and negotiating that difficulty is one of the ways in which we are called to die to the flesh in order to live to the spirit. And St Paul's remark that the letter killeth while the spirit giveth life is here highly relevant. If we refuse that death to the flesh and treat Reality and its models as one and the same, we become idolaters. For we are treating the human and relative as though it were divine and absolute, which is the quintessence of idolatry. For all our apparent zeal, for all our posing to ourselves as the loyal champions of Christian truth, we should exemplify the people described in the first chapter of Romans:

> Those who have become futile in their thinking, their senseless minds being darkened, because they have exchanged the glory of the immortal God for images resembling mortal man.

And it makes no difference whether the images are metal or mental. We *must* have images but we must sit lightly to them, and we must never confuse the images with the Reality they most inadequately represent.

We could say that Christian doctrines are symbolic representations of what is not directly accessible to our thought. And the symbolic representation has to be taken seriously but not literally.

That is another related aspect of the cross in our Christian knowledge, the tension between taking the symbol seriously but not literally. In this connection to flee from the cross is to identify seriousness with literalness so that we either take a doctrinal statement literally or abandon it altogether. That, I believe, has happened to a large extent with regard to the doctrine of Christ's second coming. Those unable to take it literally have to all intents and purposes abandoned it altogether so that it has become a vestigial remain when in fact it should be telling us things of immense importance about the relation of the historical order to eternity.

Part of the difficulty we encounter in symbolic representation is that the symbol is the product of our creative imagination, and our creative imagination needs to be held in check by our critical intelligence or discursive reason. Sometimes the one is entirely vanquished by the other. When the critical intelligence or discursive reason is entirely vanquished by the creative imagination, people will believe anything as the literal truth. The archetypes of the unconscious take over completely: evil is believed to be literally a figure with horns and a tail in command of an army of demons; monks like St Joseph of Copertino are believed to be literally capable of flying like a bird – 'Joseph flew upon an olive tree . . . A marvellous thing it was to see the branch which sustained him swaying slightly, as though a bird had alighted upon it'; statues of the Madonna are believed to weep tears. When, on the other hand, the creative imagination is entirely vanquished by the critical intelligence you get rationalizations which flatten what is held to be the truth to a level which would be intolerably dull were it not often so extremely funny: the Five Thousand are fed by everybody suddenly remembering that they have picnic baskets, an odd thing to forget when you are hungry; the divine voice at the Transfiguration was that of a man hiding behind a bush; while at Cana of Galilee, as Vincent Taylor sourly remarked, the amount of wine created was excessive for the occasion. (Would he have been more impressed if the wine had been turned into water?)

To catch a glimpse of transcendent truth in its symbolic representation, the creative imagination and the critical intelligence have to be held in continual tension. They have, like the lion and the unicorn, to chase each other round the town. Symbols are life-giving so long as it is recognized that they exist to be broken. They tell us what is in fact the case so long as we do not identify the wine of truth with the wine-skins of symbol by which it is conveyed.

One of the reasons why we need to be reminded of the necessary cross in Christian understanding is that we all have a vested interest in *not* knowing the truth, so that we take refuge in substitutes we miscall orthodoxy. One way of putting this would be to say that religious systems exist in part to protect people from the living God. There is a permanent validity in the age-old tradition that he who sees a god dies. T. S. Eliot is perhaps over-quoted: 'Human kind cannot bear very much reality.' But there is the witness of the word 'apprehend'. We apprehend the truth, but the adjective from that verb is 'apprehensive'.

But the fact of Christ means that we die in order to live. So there is no need for us to take refuge in those mental funk-holes which merely prevent our death to the flesh and our consequent entry into life. Accepting the cross of our Christian understanding in all the many and various ways in which it confronts us, we shall be raised from the dead. God will give us life and give it to us abundantly. And we shall find ourselves asking of any particular doctrine. 'To what experiences and insights does it bear witness? What good news does it seek to herald? What report about Reality is it intended to convey?'

5

PRAYER

In the last chapter I spoke of the conflicts which are involved in our Christian understanding. If we see only through a glass darkly and know only in part, that is because our doctrines about God are made up of models drawn from our experience of earthly things, and the models not only inform but misinform.

This severe limitation of the discursive reason – our ability to put two and two together and reach a conclusion – has, as we saw, always been recognized by Christian thinkers. God, they have told us, is not the answer to an intellectual problem. He is the living God with whom we can have personal communion. And the directness and simplicity of our personal communion with God has often been compared with the ambiguities and uncertainties of our attempted descriptions of Him. It is a contrast classically summed up by the author of *The Cloud of Unknowing*: 'By love God may be gotten and holden, but by thought of understanding, never.'

It looks as if we have here to do with the familiar contrast between knowledge *about* and knowledge *of*. Theological understanding gives us knowledge *about* God, but the knowledge is always so ambivalent and uncertain that it can never even begin to get a grip on Him. Knowledge *of* God is a form of love. In God's love for us and our responsive love for Him we have an immediate experience of Him which transcends thought. The contrast between knowledge about and knowledge of is in this context the contrast between theology and prayer. Transposed to the level of earthly things it is the contrast between knowing somebody intimately because we love them, and knowing all the details of their dossier while in personal terms we may know them only very slightly.

I intend in this chapter to speak about prayer. And the contrast I have just drawn between prayer and theology may make it look as if all the tensions belong to theology and none at all to prayer. But that is by no means so. Prayer has its own conflicts and there is no way of prayer which is not also the way of the cross. From one point of view conflict belongs to the very stuff of prayer.

There is, first of all, the tension between what so far I have only contrasted – prayer and theology. For the relation between these two is dialectical. To repeat an expression I have used before, prayer and theology need to chase each other round the town. Prayer is the experience of communion with God. Theology is the attempted description of that experience and its implications. But if theology thus feeds on prayer, it is also true that prayer feeds on theology. Our knowledge about God in terms of doctrine and so on, for all its blatant imperfections, provides the fuel by which alone the fire of prayer can burn. The study of theology – biblical, dogmatic, historical, philosophical, comparative, what you will – does not often feed our prayer directly. But what we learn is stored within us rather like coal in a cellar. And the time comes when the coal will be used. What we have learnt intellectually by, say, the study of a book, may be kept within us unused for a long time as far as our communion with God is concerned. But the time may come when we are ready to receive existentially what we have known so far only intellectually. And at that moment the flame of love will feed upon what so far has been only mental coal and use it to maintain and extend the fire of our communion with God. Theology and prayer thus belong together for all the contrast there is between them. Knowledge about is dead without knowledge of. But knowledge of runs into bankruptcy without a plentiful supply of knowledge about. We cannot take refuge from study by trying to be men of prayer, for study provides the food of prayer. If we were simple uneducated folk it would be different. God does not necessarily require His children to be theologians. Most of them aren't. But God always treats us as the sort of people we are. If we are educated folk (and that includes educated laymen) study for us is an essential preliminary to prayer.

In the second chapter I spoke of what I called

the analogy of feeling. God, I said, impinges upon us in terms of the kind of feelings I have towards those people to whom I am closely connected – friends, lovers, spouses, parents, and so on. It is therefore natural and inevitable that my communion with God in prayer should be experienced as an encounter or meeting with another person. The very phrase 'communion with God' suggests two people in a state of intimacy. It is not an uncommon experience for people to hold converse with God in prayer in which they appear to speak together. There is no doubt that something of God's reality is transmitted by this procedure, and we should give thanks for our ability to hold converse with God so that we speak to Him and He to us. But conflict or tension is not absent here. It is true, as I said, that something of God's reality is transmitted to us by our thus appearing to hold converse with Him. But the medium of that transmission is something not unlike a ventriloquist's dummy. For when God appears to speak to us in prayer it is we who are putting words into His mouth. We speak and the ventriloquist's dummy answers and so on. The cross of prayer here consists of accepting the humiliating fact that it is by means of something like the ventriloquist's dummy that God does in reality often get through to us, and in recognizing that in any particular instance God may not be getting through to us at all and we are left speaking only to ourselves *via* the dummy. When this possibility is not recognized the results, notoriously, can be destructive. An obvious instance is the way in which people have projected their own irrational guilt-feelings upon the heavens so that God is made to speak with the utterly unmerciful voice of a sadistic tyrant. Prayer as converse with God must involve the tension between the two possibilities of what may be going on. God may be getting through to us by means of what we make Him say or we may be doing nothing more than talking to ourselves. If we refuse to receive the tension between these two possibilities our prayer will be strangled at birth.

Another consequence follows when our communion with God is felt in terms of our encountering or meeting another. As we have seen before, towards those people with whom we are closely connected our feelings are ambivalent. However truly we love them, there will be sporadic outbursts of irritation, exasperation, wanting them to go to hell, and downright hatred, however temporary. There is at least an element of *Who's Afraid of Virginia Woolf?* in all close relationships. And, we said, the strains of a close loving relationship are most acute in the feelings an adolescent son has for his father. If we experience our communion with God as meeting another, then our feelings towards that other will have the same ambivalence, especially if we think of ourselves as God's child and of God as our Father. Yet so shocked are we at the irreverence and so ashamed of the rational absurdity of letting off our aggressions against God, that we repress them so far as God is concerned and appear to ourselves not to feel them. And then we wonder why, after we have prayed so devoutly, we feel so bloody-minded towards poor inoffensive John Smith or sweet little helpful Mary Jones or, more often, the members of our own family. Your wife, you see, has very often to have thrown at her the rotten eggs you really want to throw at God. And the joke is that God is not in the slightest degree taken in by the pantomime by which you deceive yourself. He knows what we won't admit to ourselves, that the rotten eggs are really meant for Him. When we experience God as a meeting with another to whom we are closely linked as to a father or a friend, then the ambivalence of our feelings is inevitable. It is far better to accept that fact honestly and admit it to ourselves than to repress it. There is great wisdom in Mrs Patrick Campbell's warning not to do it in the street and frighten the horses. But that prudent condition observed, if you want to blaspheme, then for Christ's sake blaspheme. If you want in your prayers to grouse, then for Christ's sake grouse. If you hate God, then for Christ's sake tell Him you do and tell Him why. He will know that these things are the necessary obverse of your love for Him and that He is Himself responsible for having made you that way. By having the courage of your aggression you will show greater trust in Him and greater love for Him than by all that 'resigned submissive meek' stuff which leaves you to take the hell out of other people, and not least out of yourself so that in consequence there is far less of you to give away.

But prayer is experienced not only as an encounter or meeting with God. It is also experienced as the discovery of our identity with Him. The tension between the experience of meeting God and finding our identity as His is so fundamental that it has been objectified into what claim to be two rival doctrines which are mutually exclusive. One doctrine says that God is other than myself. Indeed He can be described as Wholly Other. And, though only metaphorically, He is none the less considered to be very much out there. The other doctrine says that God is the ground of all things. He is the Reality present in all things. Hence He is the ground of what I myself am. He is the ocean of which I am a wave, the sun of which I am a shaft of light. My own true identity is God's identity. I am lived by God.

These two doctrines as doctrines are no doubt mutually exclusive. But each of them is no more than an attempt to solidify two distinguishable aspects of the experience of prayer: prayer as meeting God and prayer as finding He is more ourselves than we are. There is no doubt that both types of experience belong to true prayer. Sometimes we are accustomed to one and not to the other. In fact we may not know that the other exists. It is, however, important that we should know, because we may have exhausted the utility of one type of experience, at least for the time being, and we should then know where to go, that there is an alternative. Otherwise our prayer may pack up on us altogether and we may give it up.

Belonging to the West, and to the Protestant West, it is with prayer as meeting another that we shall be most familiar. (There is great truth in Norman Douglas's observation in *South Wind* that the God of northern Europe is an overseer while the God of the south is a participator.) The prayer of meeting is very rewarding and brings great riches of heart and spirit. We never outgrow it. And if we need to leave it for a time we shall certainly return to it. But we may need to leave it, at least temporarily, because for the time being it has given us all it can. We have exploited it to the point where, for the time being, it has become counter-productive. This is important enough to deserve investigation.

When in prayer we meet God as another we generally have to supply Him with clothes in order to feel His presence. We dress Him up as Heavenly Father, Mighty Saviour, Good Shepherd, the King of Love, the King of Mercy, Pity and Peace, the forgiving Friend, the wonderful Healer, the Lover,

etc., etc., etc. These clothes in which we dress
God are perfectly legitimate. It is meet and right
and indeed our duty and our joy thus to describe
God to ourselves. For the descriptions powerfully
evoke us and elicit from us wonder, love and
praise. Dwelling upon the representation of God
as Father, Saviour, Friend, and so on, we are
drawn into communion with Him. We experience
the living reality of His love, with all the praise
and worship which accompany it, by means of the
particular description of Him, by what I have
called the clothes with which we legitimately dress
Him.

But we have to be ready for various things to
happen. When we begin praying regularly, treating it as an essential part of our daily life, we may
sometimes feel that we are in love with God. The
representations with which we clothe Him evoke
strong feelings within us and the language of being
in love seems the appropriate language to describe
how we feel towards Him. Those feelings, of
course, are not so continuous as they are when we
are in love with a woman or a man. But now and
then, during the time of our prayer, we may get
the sense of God thrilling us through. It is something to thank God for and accept gratefully while
it lasts. But it must not be clutched at or
demanded. We must not try to whip ourselves up
to it artificially by psychic effort. Nor must we
imagine that something has gone wrong when
God no longer thrills us through. For, although

something of God's reality has come through to us by means of our representations of Him, it is those representations which have evoked our strong feelings. And God has a habit of detaching Himself from our representations of Him and the strong feelings they evoke. Our marvellous sensations cease. It is like ceasing to be in love with somebody and beginning to love them instead. And, although to love somebody is a far deeper, more real, and more permanent thing than being in love with them, it is also far more matter-of-fact and businesslike. Being in love is notoriously a matter of projection. We project upon the other our own ideal image and have slowly to discover that the other isn't like that. This at first leaves us feeling that we have lost something of incomparable value. But in fact we have lost nothing except the narcissistic reflection of ourselves. And what we have found is the true reality of the other and how worthy of love it is. There is a close parallel, often remarked upon, between the stages by which two people get to know and love each other and the stages by which we get to know and love God. In human relations the cross of love is a commonplace, *croce delizia*, as the operatic tenor sings. That cross has its counterpart in our love for God. 'By love God maybe gotten and holden' – true. But the surpassing glory of that love demands costly kinds of surrender.

Of these kinds of surrender the costliest has no parallel in the relation between two human beings.

It consists of the entire disappearance of God as another. God is no longer the Friend I meet, the Father with whom I hold converse, the Lover in whom I delight, the King before whom I bow in reverence, the Divine Being I worship and adore. In my experience of prayer God ceases to be any of these things because He ceases to be anything at all. He is absent when I pray. I am there alone. There is no other.

If this experience persists – and is not the effect of 'flu coming on or tiredness – it means that something of the greatest importance is happening. It means that God is inviting me to discover Him no longer as another alongside me but as my own deepest and truest self. He is calling me from the experience of meeting Him to the experience of finding my identity in Him. I cannot see Him because He is my eyes. I cannot hear Him because He is my ears. I cannot walk to Him because He is my feet. And if apparently I am alone and He is not there that is because He will not separate His presence from my own. If He is not anything at all, if He is nothing, that is because He is no longer another. I must find Him in what I am or not at all. It is difficult to put this experience of identity with God into words. It doesn't mean that God is identical with my empirical self, the self which has been highly conditioned (and no doubt distorted) by my heredity and environment, not to mention my own choices. Nor does it mean that God is identical with my ego-self with all its pretensions and selfish ambitions, the self which if intent on God says '*J'attends Dieu avec gourmandise*'. It means that there is within me a me which is both greater than me and at the same time authentically myself. One way of approaching this mysterious fact would be by what is called the paradox of grace. The more God gives me His grace (i.e. Himself), the more I am myself. The more I discover within me the greater than me, the more I discover that the greater than me is authentically me.

The initial stages of this discovery demand of us a costly surrender, a much more than little death. For what is taken from us is the warm intimacy, the loving harmony, of our meeting with the other. Our prayers appear to pack up on us completely. But here, as always, resurrection follows death, and the new life is incomparably richer than the old. For when one person meets another, however deeply they are open to each other, they still remain separated because they still remain two. They are still two islands, however plentiful and wide the bridges between them. The intimacy of personal communion only partially overcomes the split between myself as the knowing subject and the other as the known object. When my experience of prayer is that of meeting God as another, the split between subject and object remains in part at least. At the heart of my communion with God as other there is separation. But God's relation to man is not hedged in by the limitations which necessarily surround the relation

of human people to each other. In human relationships the subject–object split can be only partially
overcome. In God's relation to man the subject-
object split can be totally overcome. That is what
what we call the Incarnation is about – God and
man being one person, one identity. In this experience God is apprehended as what I myself most
deeply am, and the experience is more real than
the warmth of meeting.

It is, we believe, our final vocation and destiny
that the splendour of God in us should resplendently say, I am. But the first steps towards that
state of identity feel very far from splendid. Our
experience of identity with God is the very reverse
of what could be described as an emotional experience. It has about it no compelling grandeur which
sweeps us off our feet. Silencing ourselves for
prayer, we become aware of our identity with God
only as a dim and dull something in the back-
ground while all sorts of other things dance about
in the foreground of consciousness. Yet that dim
and dull awareness, somewhere and somehow, of
our identity with God is felt paradoxically as the
most valuable thing in our lives. It is like the grain
of mustard seed which is the smallest of all the
seeds but grows into a great tree under which
others may take cover. For around that dim and
dull awareness of our identity with God we begin,
gradually and instinctively, to centre and selve the
rest of what we are. That centring and selving
takes the whole of our life here on earth and no

doubt extends beyond the grave. But the important thing is for it to begin. And it will begin as soon as I have discovered the me in me which is greater than me, for it is around that me which is greater than me that all I am will in due time cluster and grow. Finding myself, I shall gradually make everything I am myself so that, in the end, everything I am is the presence and identity of God; to repeat the quotation from Dante: 'In us the splendour of God will resplendently say, I am,' so that God is 'engirt by what He girdeth.'

We often divide prayer up into departments: meditation or contemplation, for instance, is one department while intercession is another. From the practical point of view this division may often be necessary, but we should recognize that it is no more than a division of convenience. For our communion with God in prayer can never be for ourselves alone. I cannot enter into the presence of God only for my own sake, or only for the sake of my family, or only for the parish, or only for the Anglican communion, or only for human beings. Being human I shall naturally and rightly be more concerned for the people close to me than for others. It is stupid to try to disguise this fact from myself. I must admit it in my prayers with gratitude as human closeness is a very precious gift of God and it means that I am inevitably more concerned for John and Betty than for the diocese of Bariaboolagar and Sekfi Tumdila, the bishop. At the same time it remains true that God's presence with me is for mankind and for the universe. In prayer I put myself deliberately in the presence of God's outgoing love, and when I thus receive His outgoing love I become its agent and distributor so that through me it goes outward to all things. True prayer is thus never a form of self-culture. If his prayers make a man less interested in, less concerned about, less fellow-feeling with, the needs and agonies of the world, then there is something very wrong with his prayers. True prayer is always sacrificial in the sense that it is concerned to give and to surrender, not to get spiritual satisfactions in selfish disregard of others.

When encounter with God gives place to the discovery of my identity with Him, what I have to surrender is most of what I am accustomed to call myself: the damaged sick self we all partly are and to which we want to cling because we are obsessively fixated on the damage and sickness; the ego-image self which wants to cut a figure and make a splash even if it be only as a holy and humble man of heart; the self which feels strongly, and since it is religious, likes especially to feel God's love thrilling it through; the self bent on making progress towards spiritual maturity; the self which enjoys the rhythm of rejection and acceptance and calls it sin and repentance; the self aware of its love for God and man – all this is the self which has to be surrendered as we slowly and dimly discover our identity with God, discover the me within me which is greater than me and also authentically me. In the end we find ourselves stripped of everything except that dull, dim, rather remote awareness that we are an articulation of God's own Being, a limb of His body, to use St Paul's phrase, or, to use St John's, a branch of the vine which is Himself. Through this discovery of our true identity in God and the self-naughting which inevitably accompanies it, we become truly ourselves. And we discover that our true selves are not fixed isolated entities but are one with God's relationship to all creation. In God, we discover that we are in order that all things may be. We find ourselves caught up in God's continuous creative act as part of that act. As to be truly ourselves is to be lived by God, so God as creator puts out His own creative love as our love and our love as His.

Hence all prayer is on behalf of all things. Contemplation, because it is the discovery of who we truly are *is* intercession. For as our true selves we are God's outgoing self-givingness. We are His love.

6

ACTION

Dependence, faith, knowledge, prayer, all involve us in inner conflict. The recognition and acceptance of the conflict is our way of the cross which leads to resurrection, the losing of our life to have it more abundantly.

This chapter is concerned with the conflicts which beset us when we act.

It is obvious why there must be conflict here. Since ours is a finite existence, there are only a limited number of possibilities open to us. It is seldom that we have the chance to do the ideal thing, for we are hedged in not only by our external circumstances but also by the sort of people we are. It was of this sort of circumscription that Jesus spoke when he talked of a man wanting to build a tower who worked out the cost of it before he began building, or of a king going to war who counted his own and his enemy's army before engaging in battle. It is foolish pride to imagine that we can live beyond our spiritual income – or rather, it is foolish pride when we freely choose to try, and a fall soon follows. Of course circumstances may force us to live far beyond what we imagined was our spiritual income and thereby to be created. But that is a case of accepting the predicament that willy-nilly we find ourselves in, and discovering it is grace-bearing – something quite different from stupid, spiritually ambitious self-will which catches us up in the absurd contradiction of trying desperately to lose our life, and by this very act of trying, clutching at it frantically.

In our actions, our circumstances and disposition severely limit the number of possibilities open to us, and far from choosing to do the ideal thing we shall most often find ourselves compelled to choose between courses of action all only moderately good, or between the least of several evils. That, after all, is what Jesus had to do. He had to choose between disappearing from the scene or aggressively challenging the ecclesiastical authorities in a way which was certain to evoke their counter-aggression. And wasn't that choosing the lesser of two evils?

But our finitude not only limits the possibilities open to us. It demands of us that we do one thing rather than another. It confronts us with an either/or. That means that during our life there will be many doors accessible to us which we never opened, many roads we could have walked down but didn't. We can't, for instance, be both men of learning and also pastors available to all in need twenty-four hours a day. We can't give to our family the time they have the right to expect from us *and* live for nothing but our work. We can't both be married and be monks. And so on and so on. This necessity to choose between an either/or seems a matter of obvious common sense. But in practice it often gets loaded with a considerable degree of irrational guilt-feelings. The doors we never opened and the roads we never walked down seem to rise up and accuse us. 'Why', they complain to us, 'did you miss the opportunity of opening me? Why did you miss the opportunity of walking down me?' We hear the voice of a person in distress saying to us, 'You were so busy studying that you didn't even know I existed.' Or we hear the voice of somebody in real intellectual difficulty saying to us, 'You were so concerned to preserve your self-image as a pastor that you neglected learning and thus you were utterly useless so far as I and people like me were concerned.' If to our irrational guilt-feelings about what we chose not to do we add the common human fallacy that other fields are always greener (because we know from experience the snags involved in what we chose to do, and have no experience of the snags involved in what we didn't choose to do), taking all this into account we can begin to see the necessary cross involved in action. Even within the small circle of our limited possibilities we have to choose to do X, and choosing to do X means choosing not to do Y. And the result is both the pain of feeling guilty and the suspicion that we may well have thrown away our chances and missed the bus.

Many people try to escape from this cross by

repressing the pain it brings. The result is that they become pig-headed, obstinate, and insensitive in the bogus assurance that they have no doubts about what they do. The courageous man, on the other hand, is willing to bear his cross. He makes decisions and acts decisively once he has made up his mind, and he remains firm and consistent in his purpose. But, at the same time, he is open to new points of view and is able to see new facets of a situation because he is willing to bear the burden of his guilt-feelings and his uncertainties. He does not try to run away from them and cover them up, however decisive and consistent his actions may be. It is the combination of decisiveness with the acceptance of himself as fallible, prone to guilt-feelings and in what he decides to do certainly doing harm as well as good – it is this combination which in the realm of action marks the man of the cross.

There is too about him something of the *Pecca Fortiter*. For behind the choices he makes and the actions which follow there lie his motives. I suspect that motives for doing anything are invariably mixed, a combination of generosity and self-concern, and, even more, a combination of a me who is genuinely trying to discover and establish his true identity and a me who is running away and trying to hide from himself. Novelists of perception (Iris Murdoch comes immediately to mind) understand this game which people play with themselves. Its description is the main element in their work, so that we are always at a loss to know who the goodies are and who the baddies. If we are to make decisions and act we have to bear the burden of our mixed motives, acknowledging to ourselves that they are mixed but at the same time going ahead resolutely and acting. When we do this we shall, almost in spite of ourselves, be contributing to the ultimate fulfilment of God's purpose. As Aristotle says in his *Ethics*:

> Truly in each man's heart God lives. And God striving and spreading in him prompts him to strange actions and modes of being unaccountable even to himself. Impulses, fears, contradictions, all unreckonable. Thus under all strife it must be that the whole universe of things is striving, pursuing ever, yet not pursuing what one fancies but the One.

It is in the light of that understanding that the *Pecca Fortiter* is seen in its true significance and makes us ready to carry the cross of our own mixed motives.

It is when we engage in public, communal, political action that it is particularly important that we should know and admit to ourselves how mixed our motives are. If we believe a state of affairs is wrong, then obviously it is our duty to do what we can to have it put right, and this may well demand of us that we engage in some sort of public crusade or political campaign. Shouldn't we be running away from our vocation if we didn't?

Our politics will be a true and authentic attempt to see that right prevails in the world. To eschew politics of this kind may well be the shirking of an obvious duty. At the same time, unless we are to become fanatics, we must recognize that our devotion to the public cause has more sides to it than one. We are the champions of right over wrong: that is one very important side to it. We are seeking self-expression and self-fulfilment by means of the campaign: that is another side to it. The right we are championing is not pure transcendent right but right articulated (as it must be) in terms of a particular campaign. And there will not be general agreement about the degree in which the campaign successfully articulates the transcendent right. We shall, as always, be serving the absolute by means of the relative. That is still another side to it. The tension involved in all public political action is the necessity to act positively and boldly, to go straight for it, while at the same time realizing that our motives are mixed and that the specific campaign is only a partial and relative, and therefore inadequate, articulation of the everlasting right. If we refuse that tension we shall become either the fanatical devotees of an idol or people of such moral cowardice that we are too paralysed to campaign for the right at all. Above all, whether by temperament we are drawn to public affairs or not we must be clear that the mixed motive, the imperfect articulation of the right in practical terms, while the campaign in its methods if not its objectives will probably be a combination of wisdom and folly – we must be clear that these things do not in the slightest invalidate what people try to do by public action to make the world a better place. Scrupulosity here may merely be a disguise for laziness or simply not caring or more probably fear – the burying of our talent in the ground because we know our master is a hard man.

On the other hand, vocations will differ. And it is not for a person called predominantly to one style of life to look down upon somebody called predominantly to another. (You must forgive me if I think it is still necessary to emphasize what St Paul wrote to the Corinthians.) The public campaigner must not look down on the pastor concerned with the private and personal, nor vice versa. Nor must either of them look down on the man of prayer, nor he on them. To some extent the three will be combined in each person. Lord Shaftesbury was a man of prayer and very concerned about individuals. Somerset Ward, a great Anglican director of souls between the wars, was very aware of public issues, as his book on Robespierre shows. And Thomas Merton, the contemplative monk, was a superb pastor whose comments on the American way of life were reminiscent of the Hebrew prophets. But these all-rounders were exceptional men. In most of us there is a bit of this and a bit of that, while predominantly we are the other. We are somehow led to make a choice about our priorities. And whatever the priority we are led to choose we must recognize our dependence upon those led to choose other priorities. 'The eye cannot say to the hand, I have no need of you, nor again the head to the feet, I have no need of you' – a profound truth put out with all the charm and concealed subtlety of a Hans Andersen fairy story.

The point has now been made clear enough with regard to public activists and personalist pastors. The right of prayer to be described as an activity or called action is sometimes challenged. Indeed prayer and action are sometimes spoken of as opposites. I want to speak about that in a moment. What I want now to point out is how dependent we all are upon the activity of Christian scholars and thinkers. Personalist pastors, perhaps more than public campaigners, sometimes try (unsuccessfully) to impose a totalitarian tyranny upon scholars and thinkers. If some personalist pastors had their way the scholars and thinkers would be required to betray their loyalty to truth in order to serve up only such concoctions as the pastors assume to be spiritually healthy food for the souls in their care. The pastors often fail to see that they are trying to impose an ideology on the scholars and to rob them of their freedom in a manner exactly parallel to that used by the Soviet Politburo. The *Church Times*, for instance, took advantage of St Mark's day falling, in 1975, on their publication day to tell New Testament scholars to

be more positive in their conclusions and to allow
more of the gospels to be literal biographical truth,
as though this could be done by a political directive. There is tension, inevitably, between the
work of pastors and the work of scholars. But if
the conflict is too severe that is partly due to the
failure of the pastors to assimilate and pass on the
assured conclusions of the scholars. But still more
is it due to the trick truth is always playing upon
us in our perception of it – the trick of upsetting
the apple-cart. And the apple-cart may need to be
upset more radically and more often than a pastor
with short-term views is likely to understand. But
the tension between pastor and scholar is not
necessarily a tension between two different people.
It will often exist in the same person. His activity
as a scholar may well not harmonize too easily
with his activity as a pastor. If so, the conflict will
be most valuably creative, for as a pastor I shall
have to breathe into what in itself is only the inert
scholarly conclusion the living breath of personal
life, so that it becomes the dancing singing truth
to the person with whom I am concerned. What is
thus created has been well described by
Bonhoeffer:

> The truthful word is not in itself constant; it
> is as much alive as life itself. If it is detached
> from life and from its reference to the concrete
> other man, if 'truth is told' without taking
> into account to whom it is addressed, then

this truth has only the appearance of truth, but lacks its essential character.

Here the conflict between pastor and scholar is seen in terms of their needing each other, and of the inability of either to be himself without the other. Each needs the tension generated by the other's activity to perfect his own. The objectively truthful word becomes true truth only when account is taken of the person to whom it is addressed. And that, of course, is radically different from a political directive because the sensitivity it requires can be the fruit only of love.

Thus we come to prayer, which in essence is the cleansing of the doors of perception so that we may perceive the love in which we live and move and have our being, and assimilate it as our own. All prayer is thus activity, just as all generous activity (mixed motive and all) is a form of prayer. Prayer and action are one. To pray is a form of the verb to do, while to do is a form of the verb to pray. But the identity of prayer and action can be received by us and apprehended only in so far as we also receive and apprehend the tension between the two. Although from the ultimate point of view our being on our knees and, say, our getting a job for a man out of work are both parts of one and the same action, this fact can be recognized only if we also recognize that being on our knees is very different from taking steps to get a man a job. Unless this difference is clearly perceived and admitted, so that we spend time both on our knees and getting the job, our getting the job becomes activism, activity aimed to reassure and benefit myself under the disguise of another. But the man who needs a job is benefited either way, it could be argued. That is true in terms of our example. But the trouble with activist activity is its insensitivity, its invariable blindness to the deepest needs of the other, and a ham-fisted approach to him which makes him feel not more of a person but less. In the sphere of the Bountiful there are lords many and ladies many.

Prayer, in the sense of being on our knees, is always an activity. That is obvious when we intercede for others, and it is still fairly obvious when in our meditation our conscious mind is active as we busily think over some passage from the Bible or whatever. But it is less obvious that prayer is activity when our conscious mind is quiescent or grinds to a halt, and we apprehend God and our unity with Him at a far deeper level than that of conscious thought or identifiable feelings. Here it looks very much as if we are passive, and in a sense we are. But passivity, when it is receptive, is always action and action of a high order. Here is an example from earthly experience. Say I am musical and attend a concert. From one point of view I am totally passive. Indeed, unless I am passive, unless I cease from activity in the usual sense, the music is wasted on me. But after the concert is over I find that I am quite tired, happily

tired no doubt, but tired none the less. My tiredness shows that my passivity in the concert hall
was also a deep form of activity. To receive and
take in the music was a spending of energy. So
also in the prayer of contemplation, when the
mind and the feelings are quietened and we
become passively receptive in the presence of God,
our passivity is a deep and costly form of activity.
It is action of the highest human order which
always consists of letting go and letting God take
on. And when at prayer we are thus receptively
passively active so that we let go and let God take
on, then it inevitably colours and gives wings to
all we are and do. That is why, at regular times,
we should cease from action in the more superficial
sense in order at prayer to find that receptive
passivity which is action at its human highest
because it is the point where our letting go is God
taking on. And this in turn gives the depth of
God's own love to what we do in the ordinary
sense in the workaday world. The only real way
in which we can love and be of service to others is
to love them with God's own outgoing love. And
we need prayer to discover that we *are* God's own
outgoing love, our praying being the Holy Spirit
praying within us, and (to use Thomas Merton's
words) 'Praise praises and Thanksgiving gives
thanks'.

★ ★ ★

This letting go and letting God take on in the on-our-knees prayer has its counterpart in that wider prayer which consists of all we do in the workaday world. We have noticed how limited are the possibilities open to us and how from this limited circle of possibilities we have to choose one, and choosing one means excluding the others. All this means that we are very much hedged in, the victims very largely of necessity. The iron law of necessity operates throughout most areas of our lives. Perhaps of all the conflicts we experience, that between necessity and freedom is the most creative of all. That is more than hinted at by the arts. Art, we say, consists in limitation. If the artist is to give expression to the freedom of his insight, he must submit himself to the necessities imposed upon him by his medium, be it paint and canvas, or stone, or words, or notes. For the artist the necessity of his medium is the vehicle of his freedom. But then art is a contained affair. It is concerned with what you can do simply with paint or stone, etc. In the wide and varied jumble of our lives in general it is far harder to see necessity as the vehicle of our freedom. Yet such it is. We are hedged in by our circumstances and disposition, and our freedom consists in our relationship to them. We may shake our fist at necessity as our foe, and if we do we shall remain its victims. Or we may welcome necessity as our friend and ally, and if we do that, it will be on our side and create us.

Here inevitably we are caught up in the subsidiary tension of discovering if what we took to be necessity really is. If we can change a situation for the better, then we should change and not accept it. If I have tuberculosis I must change it into health by using the drugs for that purpose now available. In such circumstances mere acceptance of the disease would be psychopathological. But when we have discovered that a necessity is really necessary, that it is unalterable and we can do nothing to avert or change it, then our freedom consists in the acceptance of the inevitable as the medium of our creativity. It is in the very thing which compels us that we find our freedom. Great writers, for instance, have often had to write for money to support themselves and their families, and have thereby discovered the wings they possessed to soar in the freedom of their spirit. For to be free is to be fully ourselves, and it is to this becoming and being fully ourselves that we harness the hard necessities laid upon us. We make the necessity serve our purpose as persons just as the sculptor makes the hardness of the stone serve the purpose of his creative vision:

> In the deserts of the heart
> Let the healing fountain start.
> In the prison of his days
> Teach the free man how to praise.

This acceptance in our lives of necessity belongs to the highest form of action, and is a parallel to that receptive passivity which we have noted as the most valuable part of prayer. When in our lives we accept necessity which is really necessity we are letting go and letting God take on. From this highest form of human action we gradually discover that, after all, we have willed everything which has happened to us. I don't mean willing in the imperious sense of insisting that such and such is done, but the discovery that we wouldn't have had it otherwise, that there is an identity between the willed and the inevitable. What I desire is what I've got. Or as Dante put it: 'In His will is our peace.'

7

CONFLICT
RESOLVED

Our theme in this book has been the way of the cross, that losing of our life to find it which takes the form of those necessary and health-giving conflicts which are the price we have to pay for becoming more fully ourselves. The necessity of dependence has to fight with the necessity of autonomy, the necessity of faith with the necessity of doubt. True knowledge consists of the realization that not knowing is inseparably bound up with every act of knowing. In prayer what is revealed to us is both the otherness of God and also our identity with Him. We act as those to whom necessity is their freedom, while passivity as receptiveness is the highest form of activity.

Involved in conflicts of this kind – and sleep or death are the only alternatives – it looks as if being alive and growing is a pretty tough business. And so it is. The pilgrim's progress towards the Celestial City is no easy promenade, nor can it be done in some luxury coach of total resignation or complete certainty or perfect knowledge or some absolute dream of a prayer. We have to slog along on foot, and the most taxing thing about the path is neither its roughness nor its steepness but the fact that, as Jesus said, it's so narrow. Indeed it is often a knife-edge, as we have seen.

But for all the conflicts and tensions we mustn't forget the Delectable Mountains from which we see the Celestial City, if only from afar. Bunyan's picture of the Delectable Mountains is one of the most marvellous in *Pilgrim's Progress* . In terms of Bunyan's story the Delectable Mountains had to be one stage on the road, a temporary resting-place reached when Christian's journey was already more than half over, and which was left behind when the time came to move on. But in life, wherever else we are, we are always also on the Delectable Mountains from which we can catch a glimpse of the Celestial City, the city which is the object of our quest because we know somewhere, somehow, that it is the place where we most truly belong. And while our glimpse of the city lasts, we are at rest. The necessary conflicts of our life are for the time being resolved. And we experience a foretaste of their final and permanent resolution.

It is therefore of the Delectable Mountains that I intend to speak in this last chapter.

The Delectable Mountains can take as many forms as there are people. Your own particular experience of them will not be exactly identical with that of anybody else, since you are a unique person with a unique destiny. Obviously therefore we must go not for the particular but for the general; each person will have his own unique experience of the Delectable Mountains, but we must go for the experience which is common to us all. Some of us are married, some aren't. Some of us are capable of intellectual satisfactions, some aren't. To some of us music reveals Reality, to others it doesn't. Some of us take to religion like a duck to water, others (I am one of them) find it all but intolerable. I have known people to whom rowing in an eight is a mystical experience. There is no need to labour the point further. What we need is a description of the Delectable Mountains which is common to everybody, whoever they are and whatever their talents, predilections or circumstances. If people catch a glimpse of their conflicts resolved, what is the universal form of that vision?

I suggest that it is laughter.

I mean real laughter at what is seen as inherently funny. What is the test of real laughter? It is the ability to see the funny side of your own situation, the ability to laugh at yourself as well as about other people. Without the ability to laugh at yourself, to find delighted pleasure in the comic aspects of your own character and circumstances, laughter becomes perverted: a superior sneer, a transparent disguise for cynicism and defeat, a defence mechanism to give to others and yourself the impression that you are more at ease and less frightened than in fact you are – committee laughter, cocktail-party laughter, self-consciously

Christian laughter: 'We may be dead but by God we can be cheerful.' A man who laughs at himself, who enjoys the fun of being what he is, does not fall into the perversion of laughter. Mirth, like charity, has to begin at home if it is to be genuine.

In one of Christopher Fry's plays an ageing couple talk of decay and mortality. 'Shall we laugh?' asks the man. 'For what reason?' asks the woman. 'For the reason of laughter,' is the reply, 'since laughter is surely the surest touch of genius in creation. Would *you* ever have thought of it? That same laughter, madam, is an irrelevancy which almost amounts to revelation.'

God, we believe, accepts us, accepts all men, unconditionally, warts and all. Laughter is the purest form of our response to God's acceptance of us. For when I laugh at myself I accept myself and when I laugh at other people in genuine mirth I accept them. Self-acceptance in laughter is the very opposite of self-satisfaction or pride. For in laughter I accept myself not because I'm some sort of super-person, but precisely because I'm not. There is nothing funny about a super-person. There is everything funny about a man who thinks he is. In laughing at my own claims to importance or regard I receive myself in a sort of loving forgiveness which is an echo of God's forgiveness of me. In much conventional contrition there is a selfishness and pride which are scarcely hidden. In our desperate self-concern we blame ourselves for not being the super-persons we think we really are. But in laughter we sit light to ourselves. That is why laughter is the purest form of our response to God. Whether or not the great saints were capable of levitation, I have not the evidence to decide. What I do know is that a characteristic of the great saints is their power of levity. For to sit light to yourself is true humility. Pride cannot rise to levity. As G. K. Chesterton said, pride is the downward drag of all things into an easy solemnity. It would seem that a heavy seriousness is as natural to man as falling. 'It was by the force of gravity that Satan fell.' Laughter, on the other hand, is a sign of grace.

Nowhere in all literature is this point put more devastatingly or more poignantly than in *King Lear*. From the start Lear takes himself with the utmost seriousness. His pride makes him utterly blind and leads him to actions which drive him to insanity and destruction. If only he could see the joke he would be saved. But he can't. Yet the Fool tries continually to make him see it, and Lear's self-imprisonment in a situation where humour is so totally out of place as to be obscene is one of the most horrific aspects of the play. Lear is in hell because he has made laughter loathesomely inappropriate. His egotistical self-dramatization as the most generous of fathers has led two of his daughters to disown him. And he says to the Fool: 'When were you wont to be so full of songs, sirrah?' To which the Fool answers: 'I have used it, nuncle, ever since thou madest thy daughters thy mothers': ever since 'thou gavest them the rod and put'st down thine own breeches.' Or when in madness Lear tears off his clothes, the Fool says: 'Prithee, nuncle, be contented: 'tis a naughty night to swim in.' If in the intolerable grimness of his self-inflicted torture Lear could have risen to the merest flicker of a laugh, he would have been a man redeemed. The pride which from the first has made him incapable of laughter is the essence of his appalling tragedy.

So, from the bottom of your heart thank God when you can see the joke popping out of your circumstances, even when they are grim. Thank God when you can take a delighted pleasure in the comic spectacle which is yourself, especially if it is yourself devoutly at prayer. (Why am I like a famous jackdaw?) Thank God when you can laugh. It means that you are on the Delectable Mountains and that your redemption has drawn nigh.

In my second chapter I quoted one or two ancient rabbis. Let me now tell a story of a more recent one, quoted in an essay by W. H. Auden:

In Lublin lived a great sinner. Whenever he went to talk to the rabbi, the rabbi readily consented and conversed with him as if he were a man of integrity and one who was a close friend. Many of the hassidim were annoyed at this and one said to the other: 'Is it possible that our rabbi who has only to look once into a man's face to know his life from first to last, to know the very origin of his soul, does not see that this fellow is a sinner? And if he does see it, that he considers him worthy to speak to and associate with?' Finally they summoned up courage to go to the rabbi himself with their question. He answered them: 'I know all about him as well as you. But you know how I love gaiety and hate dejection. And this man is so great a sinner. Others repent the moment they have sinned, are sorry for a moment, and then return to their folly. But he knows no regrets and no doldrums, and lives in his happiness as in a tower. And it is the radiance of his happiness that overwhelms my heart.'

Clearly, as the rabbi saw, the sinner of Lublin lived on the Delectable Mountains. He was a scamp, no doubt. But he was also the beggar of grace. His invincible merriment showed him to belong to what the theologians call the supernatural order of charity. And if that example of the last being first makes you as indignant as those labourers in the vineyard who had borne the burden and heat of the day, well then, your indignation is very funny too.

If by laughter I accept myself, it is by laughter that I also accept others. Everybody has warts. The only alternatives are to get angry about the warts or to laugh about them. To pretend that they don't exist is to be like the courtier in the fairy story who heard a cow mooing, and thinking it was the Princess, said: 'Listen, how beautifully she sings.' But laughter is realistic. It is an acceptance of somebody warts and all. 'Real laughter is absolutely unaggressive; we cannot wish people we find amusing to be other than they are; we do not desire to change them, far less to hurt or destroy them' (Auden). It is, for instance, always Mrs Malaprop who gets the loudest applause at the end of the play. In the very absurdity of her idiotic intellectual pretensions she is revealed as lovable somehow. Sheridan's achievement is to give us eyes to recognize the Mrs Malaprops we meet off-stage and in our laughter to love them.

And another very important thing to notice is that in the love which is laughter we never try to get something for ourselves on the sly from the people we think we love. The most common perversion of love is a disguised acquisitiveness, a possessiveness which murders love. But a love which laughs is never possessive or on the make. It is too delighted with the caperings of the other person to have any time to think of itself. 'That is why a man in a passion of any kind cannot be made to laugh. If he laughs, it is a proof that his passion has been dissipated' (Auden).

Altogether, I suggest that laughter is the best and clearest reflection we ever get in this world of

God's love for His creation. In laughter we see the Celestial City in what is more than a passing glimpse.

So far, however, we have been considering laughter only in our personal relations – with ourselves and with others. But laughter has also a metaphysical dimension, by which I mean that it is closely bound up with our most fundamental beliefs and deepest commitments. Those necessary conflicts which have been the concern of this book derive very largely from the fact that we have to live on several different levels of being at the same time. And the levels inevitably clash with each other. A man may on one level, for instance, have a sturdy independence of character while on another level he may be utterly dependent. I forget of what Roman emperor it was said that he was a great leader of men and follower of women. Another man may have the deepest faith in God's perpetual Providence and be terrified in an aeroplane. There are clever fools and unlearned philosophers. There are hard-headed businessmen who will weep at the death of Mimi each time they see her die. There are men of prayer who are almost suicidal if they miss a train. Such incongruities between the various levels of our existence are the very essence of humour, and when we perceive them we can't help laughing. The situation is made all the more comic by the fact that each level of our existence is some sort of self-consistent whole. If we keep within the limits of one particular level, then everything fits together neatly – neatly enough, indeed, to be positively dull. But bring in another level of existence, and the clash between the two independent self-consistent levels makes everything go haywire. During the war, for instance, Stalin once asked Churchill how many troops were at the disposal of the Vatican. To which Churchill replied: 'Several legions, not all of them visible on parade.' The juxtaposition of time and eternity is always laughable. I found the converse of the Churchill story in a Christmas number of the *New Yorker*: there was a drawing of the stable at Bethlehem with the caption, 'But we wanted a girl.' Necessity and contingency are indeed very odd bedfellows. And that is the whole glory – and the whole joke – of Christian faith. Our experience drives us to believe two completely opposite things at once, and what, in the last resort, can we do but laugh at the sheer ludicrous fun of it all?

In terms of time the eternal Lord of all order appears to be the Lord of misrule. No wonder the pharisees, who seem to have been always wholly serious, had to have Jesus put down. He couldn't be allowed to go on indefinitely standing everything on its head and making their piety look ridiculous. Why, in the end, they might even laugh themselves, and that would be the ultimate catastrophe. Who in reality had ever witnessed a pious man blowing a trumpet before he put a pound note in the church box? The notion was irresponsibly misleading. And then there were camels going through the eyes of needles, not to mention camels being swallowed easily by those who choked when they swallowed a gnat. And if people did sometimes get a speck in their eye who ever heard of a man, and an improving teacher at that, who had a log in his? And worse: idlers who were given full pay, stewards who were successful cheats, spendthrift and debauched sons being fêted on their return home – what had all this pernicious nonsense to do with religion? It could only undermine the morals of society, and, being socially dangerous, had to be stopped; stopped before the contagion of eternal love showed up the whole solemn system of moralism and religiosity as a complete knockabout farce. So the Jester had to be crucified.

But Eternity had the last laugh after all. For that is the final joke – the resurrection. Here are Caiaphas and all his crowd, Pilate and Herod and all theirs, sitting complacently in a state of grave and dignified self-congratulation. They have done their duty and justified the authority vested in them by efficiently disposing once for all of a dangerous fool. He is safely dead. And with solemn calm again restored they can concentrate once more on the really serious matters to which their lives are dedicated. But behind their backs, without them having the slightest inkling of what is going on, the fool has popped up again like a Jack-in-the-box and is dancing about even more vigorously than before and even more compellingly. People here, there and everywhere are falling under his spell. But the brass hats and mitred heads and stuffed shirts are facing the other way and can't see what is going on. So they continue with their dignified mutual congratulation and their serious business.

If that isn't funny, nothing is. It is the supreme, the final, the ultimate joke – that than which nothing could be funnier. And since laughter, although not irresistible is none the less highly contagious, perhaps the brass hats themselves will in time catch the disease, turn round, see the joke, and laugh with the rest of creation because the kingdom of God has drawn near.

And the fun continues in heaven which, as Julian of Norwich said, is right merry. Perhaps – who knows? – we shall see Athanasius and Arius laughing together at the absurdity of their theological definitions; or Augustine and Pelagius slapping each other on the back instead of in the face. We may even see Mr Gladstone enormously and unashamedly enjoying the company of those he has mistaken for fallen angels. But the best of it will be those white robes supplied by the celestial Moss Bros, because they certainly won't fit and we shall all look like dustmen got up as dukes. And the fun of that will make the party go with a bang.

* * *

On the Delectable Mountains of laughter we sense the glory which shall be revealed in us. Indeed we know the glory is already ours, and that is what makes our present ragamuffin state so deliciously ludicrous. At Mirfield in our Community church we sit in order of seniority. The places occupied by the oldest men are known as Cemetery Row. 'I see you've been moved up to Cemetery Row', we say to an elder brother. That Community joke makes the hottest kind of evangelism look by contrast like the negation of God. For through the joke of Cemetery Row there rings the laughter of the universe, and there isn't much laughter in hot gospel unless you see how funny it is.

The incongruity between death and fullness of life gathers up all the other incongruities, all the contradictions, conflicts, and tensions which in this world must be not only accepted but positively welcomed and joyfully received. For it is only when we thus welcome and receive them that we discover, when all is said and done, how laughable they are. And although we are still on our journey, when we laugh we know that really we have already arrived. The party has begun and we are there.

Fount Paperbacks

Fount is one of the leading paperback publishers of religious books and below are some of its recent titles.

☐ **THROUGH SEASONS OF THE HEART**
John Powell   £4.95
☐ **WORDS OF LIFE FROM JOHN THE BELOVED**
Frances Hogan   £2.95
☐ **MEISTER ECKHART** Ursula Fleming   £2.95
☐ **CHASING THE WILD GOOSE** Ron Ferguson   £2.95
☐ **A GOOD HARVEST** Rita Snowden   £2.50
☐ **UNFINISHED ENCOUNTER** Bob Whyte   £5.95
☐ **FIRST STEPS IN PRAYER** Jean-Marie Lustiger   £2.95
☐ **IF THIS IS TREASON** Allan Boesak   £2.95
☐ **RECLAIMING THE CHURCH** Robin Greenwood   £2.95
☐ **GOD WITHIN US** John Wijngaards   £2.95
☐ **GOD'S WORLD** Trevor Huddleston   £2.95
☐ **A CALL TO WITNESS** Oliver McTernan   £2.95
☐ **GOODNIGHT LORD** Georgette Butcher   £2.95
☐ **FOR GOD'S SAKE** Donald Reeves   £3.50
☐ **GROWING OLDER** Una Kroll   £2.95
☐ **THROUGH THE YEAR WITH FRANCIS OF ASSISI**
Murray Bodo   £2.95

All Fount Paperbacks are available at your bookshop or newsagent, or they can be ordered by post from Fount Paperbacks, Cash Sales Department, G.P.O. Box 29, Douglas, Isle of Man. Please send purchase price plus 22p per book, maximum postage £3. Customers outside the UK send purchase price, plus 22p per book. Cheque, postal order or money order. No currency.

NAME (Block letters) _____

ADDRESS_____

_____

_____

While every effort is made to keep prices low, it is sometimes necessary to increase them at short notice. Fount Paperbacks reserve the right to show new retail prices on covers which may differ from those previously advertised in the text or elsewhere.